Family History Record Book 2

A FAMILY TREE WORKBOOK EXTENSION TO RECORD GENERATIONS 9 & 10

H
heritagehunter

Find other history publications at
www.heritagehunter.co.uk

ISBN 978-1-905315-35-2 (paperback)
ISBN 978-1-905315-36-9 (hardback)

Sign up for the free Histories newsletter at
www.gethistories.com

How to use this book

Keeping track of your family history can soon get tricky as the amount of information you gather about each ancestor builds up. This book provides you with an easy way to keep all of this information in one place – this makes it ideal for a summary of your research which you can carry with you if you are visiting archives and libraries, and indeed a great way to share your family history with relatives for posterity.

Note: this book is a companion to the earlier Family History Record Book (available from Amazon and other online retailers, as well as www.heritagehunter.co.uk) and is best used alongside it. The first book covers eight generations (from you back to your 5x-great-grandparents) – this book provides space to record details for two further generations back in time, ie up to your 7x-great-grandparents. Used together, the books can record details of more than 1000 ancestors!

This volume has two main sections. The first, covering pages iv to xix, provides an opportunity to record an at-a-glance summary of your direct ancestors, from the eighth generation (the furthest extent of the previous volume) to the tenth. Then each subsequent page provides space for one of your 6x-great-grandparents *and* their two parents.

You'll see that every single person in your tree of ancestors has been allocated a number, shown in bold – this is known in genealogy as an Ahnentafel number (see https://www.thoughtco.com/ahnentafel-numbering-system-explained-1420744, for example). It's very simple to use: to find any person's father, simply double their number – and to find their mother, double it and add one. Or, of course, conversely, you can go down the generations by halving (take away one from an add number first). This means that all even numbers represent male ancestors, and odd numbers female ones (number 1 is reserved for you or any other starting individual, and can be either male or female). Male ancestors are also indicated with a gray tint.

So the second part of this book allocates half a page to each of your 256 forebears of the ninth generation (where you count as the first) AND two of your 512 tenth-generation ones. You can use the bold numbers to find an individual quickly, and of course all this cross-references with the summary pages in the first part of the book. And these numbers in this book cover the overall generations:

5x-great-grandparents	128–255
6x-great-grandparents	256–511
(your paternal ancestors 256–383; maternal 384–511)	
7x-great-grandparents	512–1023
(your paternal ancestors 512–767; maternal 768–1023)	

For each individual, you can note down your key pieces of information, organised by date, the source of the information (eg census, parish record, specific archive, etc) and the actual details – there's room for numerous items per person, and of course these can include anything from vital dates to occupations, siblings, children born or where they lived.

5x-great-grandparents

128 Name:
B: / / M: / / D: / /

129 Name:
B: / / M: / / D: / /

130 Name:
B: / / M: / / D: / /

131 Name:
B: / / M: / / D: / /

132 Name:
B: / / M: / / D: / /

133 Name:
B: / / M: / / D: / /

134 Name:
B: / / M: / / D: / /

135 Name:
B: / / M: / / D: / /

136 Name:
B: / / M: / / D: / /

137 Name:
B: / / M: / / D: / /

138 Name:
B: / / M: / / D: / /

139 Name:
B: / / M: / / D: / /

140 Name:
B: / / M: / / D: / /

141 Name:
B: / / M: / / D: / /

142 Name:
B: / / M: / / D: / /

143 Name:
B: / / M: / / D: / /

6x-great-grandparents

256 Name: B:_/_/_ M:_/_/_ D:_/_/_

257 Name: B:_/_/_ M:_/_/_ D:_/_/_

258 Name: B:_/_/_ M:_/_/_ D:_/_/_

259 Name: B:_/_/_ M:_/_/_ D:_/_/_

260 Name: B:_/_/_ M:_/_/_ D:_/_/_

261 Name: B:_/_/_ M:_/_/_ D:_/_/_

262 Name: B:_/_/_ M:_/_/_ D:_/_/_

263 Name: B:_/_/_ M:_/_/_ D:_/_/_

264 Name: B:_/_/_ M:_/_/_ D:_/_/_

265 Name: B:_/_/_ M:_/_/_ D:_/_/_

266 Name: B:_/_/_ M:_/_/_ D:_/_/_

267 Name: B:_/_/_ M:_/_/_ D:_/_/_

268 Name: B:_/_/_ M:_/_/_ D:_/_/_

269 Name: B:_/_/_ M:_/_/_ D:_/_/_

270 Name: B:_/_/_ M:_/_/_ D:_/_/_

271 Name: B:_/_/_ M:_/_/_ D:_/_/_

272 Name: B:_/_/_ M:_/_/_ D:_/_/_

273 Name: B:_/_/_ M:_/_/_ D:_/_/_

274 Name: B:_/_/_ M:_/_/_ D:_/_/_

275 Name: B:_/_/_ M:_/_/_ D:_/_/_

276 Name: B:_/_/_ M:_/_/_ D:_/_/_

277 Name: B:_/_/_ M:_/_/_ D:_/_/_

278 Name: B:_/_/_ M:_/_/_ D:_/_/_

279 Name: B:_/_/_ M:_/_/_ D:_/_/_

280 Name: B:_/_/_ M:_/_/_ D:_/_/_

281 Name: B:_/_/_ M:_/_/_ D:_/_/_

282 Name: B:_/_/_ M:_/_/_ D:_/_/_

283 Name: B:_/_/_ M:_/_/_ D:_/_/_

284 Name: B:_/_/_ M:_/_/_ D:_/_/_

285 Name: B:_/_/_ M:_/_/_ D:_/_/_

286 Name: B:_/_/_ M:_/_/_ D:_/_/_

287 Name: B:_/_/_ M:_/_/_ D:_/_/_

7X-GREAT-GRANDPARENTS (MALE)		7X-GREAT-GRANDPARENTS (FEMALE)
512 Name: B:_/_/_ M:_/_/_ D:_/_/_	&	**513** Name: B:_/_/_ M:_/_/_ D:_/_/_
514 Name: B:_/_/_ M:_/_/_ D:_/_/_	&	**515** Name: B:_/_/_ M:_/_/_ D:_/_/_
516 Name: B:_/_/_ M:_/_/_ D:_/_/_	&	**517** Name: B:_/_/_ M:_/_/_ D:_/_/_
518 Name: B:_/_/_ M:_/_/_ D:_/_/_	&	**519** Name: B:_/_/_ M:_/_/_ D:_/_/_
520 Name: B:_/_/_ M:_/_/_ D:_/_/_	&	**521** Name: B:_/_/_ M:_/_/_ D:_/_/_
522 Name: B:_/_/_ M:_/_/_ D:_/_/_	&	**523** Name: B:_/_/_ M:_/_/_ D:_/_/_
524 Name: B:_/_/_ M:_/_/_ D:_/_/_	&	**525** Name: B:_/_/_ M:_/_/_ D:_/_/_
526 Name: B:_/_/_ M:_/_/_ D:_/_/_	&	**527** Name: B:_/_/_ M:_/_/_ D:_/_/_
528 Name: B:_/_/_ M:_/_/_ D:_/_/_	&	**529** Name: B:_/_/_ M:_/_/_ D:_/_/_
530 Name: B:_/_/_ M:_/_/_ D:_/_/_	&	**531** Name: B:_/_/_ M:_/_/_ D:_/_/_
532 Name: B:_/_/_ M:_/_/_ D:_/_/_	&	**533** Name: B:_/_/_ M:_/_/_ D:_/_/_
534 Name: B:_/_/_ M:_/_/_ D:_/_/_	&	**535** Name: B:_/_/_ M:_/_/_ D:_/_/_
536 Name: B:_/_/_ M:_/_/_ D:_/_/_	&	**537** Name: B:_/_/_ M:_/_/_ D:_/_/_
538 Name: B:_/_/_ M:_/_/_ D:_/_/_	&	**539** Name: B:_/_/_ M:_/_/_ D:_/_/_
540 Name: B:_/_/_ M:_/_/_ D:_/_/_	&	**541** Name: B:_/_/_ M:_/_/_ D:_/_/_
542 Name: B:_/_/_ M:_/_/_ D:_/_/_	&	**543** Name: B:_/_/_ M:_/_/_ D:_/_/_
544 Name: B:_/_/_ M:_/_/_ D:_/_/_	&	**545** Name: B:_/_/_ M:_/_/_ D:_/_/_
546 Name: B:_/_/_ M:_/_/_ D:_/_/_	&	**547** Name: B:_/_/_ M:_/_/_ D:_/_/_
548 Name: B:_/_/_ M:_/_/_ D:_/_/_	&	**549** Name: B:_/_/_ M:_/_/_ D:_/_/_
550 Name: B:_/_/_ M:_/_/_ D:_/_/_	&	**551** Name: B:_/_/_ M:_/_/_ D:_/_/_
552 Name: B:_/_/_ M:_/_/_ D:_/_/_	&	**553** Name: B:_/_/_ M:_/_/_ D:_/_/_
554 Name: B:_/_/_ M:_/_/_ D:_/_/_	&	**555** Name: B:_/_/_ M:_/_/_ D:_/_/_
556 Name: B:_/_/_ M:_/_/_ D:_/_/_	&	**557** Name: B:_/_/_ M:_/_/_ D:_/_/_
558 Name: B:_/_/_ M:_/_/_ D:_/_/_	&	**559** Name: B:_/_/_ M:_/_/_ D:_/_/_
560 Name: B:_/_/_ M:_/_/_ D:_/_/_	&	**561** Name: B:_/_/_ M:_/_/_ D:_/_/_
562 Name: B:_/_/_ M:_/_/_ D:_/_/_	&	**563** Name: B:_/_/_ M:_/_/_ D:_/_/_
564 Name: B:_/_/_ M:_/_/_ D:_/_/_	&	**565** Name: B:_/_/_ M:_/_/_ D:_/_/_
566 Name: B:_/_/_ M:_/_/_ D:_/_/_	&	**567** Name: B:_/_/_ M:_/_/_ D:_/_/_
568 Name: B:_/_/_ M:_/_/_ D:_/_/_	&	**569** Name: B:_/_/_ M:_/_/_ D:_/_/_
570 Name: B:_/_/_ M:_/_/_ D:_/_/_	&	**571** Name: B:_/_/_ M:_/_/_ D:_/_/_
572 Name: B:_/_/_ M:_/_/_ D:_/_/_	&	**573** Name: B:_/_/_ M:_/_/_ D:_/_/_
574 Name: B:_/_/_ M:_/_/_ D:_/_/_	&	**575** Name: B:_/_/_ M:_/_/_ D:_/_/_

For previous generations, see previous Family History Record Book

5X-GREAT-GRANDPARENTS

144 Name:
B: / / M: / / D: / /

145 Name:
B: / / M: / / D: / /

146 Name:
B: / / M: / / D: / /

147 Name:
B: / / M: / / D: / /

148 Name:
B: / / M: / / D: / /

149 Name:
B: / / M: / / D: / /

150 Name:
B: / / M: / / D: / /

151 Name:
B: / / M: / / D: / /

152 Name:
B: / / M: / / D: / /

153 Name:
B: / / M: / / D: / /

154 Name:
B: / / M: / / D: / /

155 Name:
B: / / M: / / D: / /

156 Name:
B: / / M: / / D: / /

157 Name:
B: / / M: / / D: / /

158 Name:
B: / / M: / / D: / /

159 Name:
B: / / M: / / D: / /

6X-GREAT-GRANDPARENTS

288 Name: B:_/_/_ M:_/_/_ D:_/_/_

289 Name: B:_/_/_ M:_/_/_ D:_/_/_

290 Name: B:_/_/_ M:_/_/_ D:_/_/_

291 Name: B:_/_/_ M:_/_/_ D:_/_/_

292 Name: B:_/_/_ M:_/_/_ D:_/_/_

293 Name: B:_/_/_ M:_/_/_ D:_/_/_

294 Name: B:_/_/_ M:_/_/_ D:_/_/_

295 Name: B:_/_/_ M:_/_/_ D:_/_/_

296 Name: B:_/_/_ M:_/_/_ D:_/_/_

297 Name: B:_/_/_ M:_/_/_ D:_/_/_

298 Name: B:_/_/_ M:_/_/_ D:_/_/_

299 Name: B:_/_/_ M:_/_/_ D:_/_/_

300 Name: B:_/_/_ M:_/_/_ D:_/_/_

301 Name: B:_/_/_ M:_/_/_ D:_/_/_

302 Name: B:_/_/_ M:_/_/_ D:_/_/_

303 Name: B:_/_/_ M:_/_/_ D:_/_/_

304 Name: B:_/_/_ M:_/_/_ D:_/_/_

305 Name: B:_/_/_ M:_/_/_ D:_/_/_

306 Name: B:_/_/_ M:_/_/_ D:_/_/_

307 Name: B:_/_/_ M:_/_/_ D:_/_/_

308 Name: B:_/_/_ M:_/_/_ D:_/_/_

309 Name: B:_/_/_ M:_/_/_ D:_/_/_

310 Name: B:_/_/_ M:_/_/_ D:_/_/_

311 Name: B:_/_/_ M:_/_/_ D:_/_/_

312 Name: B:_/_/_ M:_/_/_ D:_/_/_

313 Name: B:_/_/_ M:_/_/_ D:_/_/_

314 Name: B:_/_/_ M:_/_/_ D:_/_/_

315 Name: B:_/_/_ M:_/_/_ D:_/_/_

316 Name: B:_/_/_ M:_/_/_ D:_/_/_

317 Name: B:_/_/_ M:_/_/_ D:_/_/_

318 Name: B:_/_/_ M:_/_/_ D:_/_/_

319 Name: B:_/_/_ M:_/_/_ D:_/_/_

7X-GREAT-GRANDPARENTS (MALE)		7X-GREAT-GRANDPARENTS (FEMALE)
576 Name: B:_/_/_ M:_/_/_ D:_/_/_	&	577 Name: B:_/_/_ M:_/_/_ D:_/_/_
578 Name: B:_/_/_ M:_/_/_ D:_/_/_	&	579 Name: B:_/_/_ M:_/_/_ D:_/_/_
580 Name: B:_/_/_ M:_/_/_ D:_/_/_	&	581 Name: B:_/_/_ M:_/_/_ D:_/_/_
582 Name: B:_/_/_ M:_/_/_ D:_/_/_	&	583 Name: B:_/_/_ M:_/_/_ D:_/_/_
584 Name: B:_/_/_ M:_/_/_ D:_/_/_	&	585 Name: B:_/_/_ M:_/_/_ D:_/_/_
586 Name: B:_/_/_ M:_/_/_ D:_/_/_	&	587 Name: B:_/_/_ M:_/_/_ D:_/_/_
588 Name: B:_/_/_ M:_/_/_ D:_/_/_	&	589 Name: B:_/_/_ M:_/_/_ D:_/_/_
590 Name: B:_/_/_ M:_/_/_ D:_/_/_	&	591 Name: B:_/_/_ M:_/_/_ D:_/_/_
592 Name: B:_/_/_ M:_/_/_ D:_/_/_	&	593 Name: B:_/_/_ M:_/_/_ D:_/_/_
594 Name: B:_/_/_ M:_/_/_ D:_/_/_	&	595 Name: B:_/_/_ M:_/_/_ D:_/_/_
596 Name: B:_/_/_ M:_/_/_ D:_/_/_	&	597 Name: B:_/_/_ M:_/_/_ D:_/_/_
598 Name: B:_/_/_ M:_/_/_ D:_/_/_	&	599 Name: B:_/_/_ M:_/_/_ D:_/_/_
600 Name: B:_/_/_ M:_/_/_ D:_/_/_	&	601 Name: B:_/_/_ M:_/_/_ D:_/_/_
602 Name: B:_/_/_ M:_/_/_ D:_/_/_	&	603 Name: B:_/_/_ M:_/_/_ D:_/_/_
604 Name: B:_/_/_ M:_/_/_ D:_/_/_	&	605 Name: B:_/_/_ M:_/_/_ D:_/_/_
606 Name: B:_/_/_ M:_/_/_ D:_/_/_	&	607 Name: B:_/_/_ M:_/_/_ D:_/_/_
608 Name: B:_/_/_ M:_/_/_ D:_/_/_	&	609 Name: B:_/_/_ M:_/_/_ D:_/_/_
610 Name: B:_/_/_ M:_/_/_ D:_/_/_	&	611 Name: B:_/_/_ M:_/_/_ D:_/_/_
612 Name: B:_/_/_ M:_/_/_ D:_/_/_	&	613 Name: B:_/_/_ M:_/_/_ D:_/_/_
614 Name: B:_/_/_ M:_/_/_ D:_/_/_	&	615 Name: B:_/_/_ M:_/_/_ D:_/_/_
616 Name: B:_/_/_ M:_/_/_ D:_/_/_	&	617 Name: B:_/_/_ M:_/_/_ D:_/_/_
618 Name: B:_/_/_ M:_/_/_ D:_/_/_	&	619 Name: B:_/_/_ M:_/_/_ D:_/_/_
620 Name: B:_/_/_ M:_/_/_ D:_/_/_	&	621 Name: B:_/_/_ M:_/_/_ D:_/_/_
622 Name: B:_/_/_ M:_/_/_ D:_/_/_	&	623 Name: B:_/_/_ M:_/_/_ D:_/_/_
624 Name: B:_/_/_ M:_/_/_ D:_/_/_	&	625 Name: B:_/_/_ M:_/_/_ D:_/_/_
626 Name: B:_/_/_ M:_/_/_ D:_/_/_	&	627 Name: B:_/_/_ M:_/_/_ D:_/_/_
628 Name: B:_/_/_ M:_/_/_ D:_/_/_	&	629 Name: B:_/_/_ M:_/_/_ D:_/_/_
630 Name: B:_/_/_ M:_/_/_ D:_/_/_	&	631 Name: B:_/_/_ M:_/_/_ D:_/_/_
632 Name: B:_/_/_ M:_/_/_ D:_/_/_	&	633 Name: B:_/_/_ M:_/_/_ D:_/_/_
634 Name: B:_/_/_ M:_/_/_ D:_/_/_	&	635 Name: B:_/_/_ M:_/_/_ D:_/_/_
636 Name: B:_/_/_ M:_/_/_ D:_/_/_	&	637 Name: B:_/_/_ M:_/_/_ D:_/_/_
638 Name: B:_/_/_ M:_/_/_ D:_/_/_	&	639 Name: B:_/_/_ M:_/_/_ D:_/_/_

For previous generations, see previous Family History Record Book

5x-great-grandparents

160 Name:
B: / / M: / / D: / /

161 Name:
B: / / M: / / D: / /

162 Name:
B: / / M: / / D: / /

163 Name:
B: / / M: / / D: / /

164 Name:
B: / / M: / / D: / /

165 Name:
B: / / M: / / D: / /

166 Name:
B: / / M: / / D: / /

167 Name:
B: / / M: / / D: / /

168 Name:
B: / / M: / / D: / /

169 Name:
B: / / M: / / D: / /

170 Name:
B: / / M: / / D: / /

171 Name:
B: / / M: / / D: / /

172 Name:
B: / / M: / / D: / /

173 Name:
B: / / M: / / D: / /

174 Name:
B: / / M: / / D: / /

175 Name:
B: / / M: / / D: / /

6x-great-grandparents

320 Name: B:_/_/_ M:_/_/_ D:_/_/_

321 Name: B:_/_/_ M:_/_/_ D:_/_/_

322 Name: B:_/_/_ M:_/_/_ D:_/_/_

323 Name: B:_/_/_ M:_/_/_ D:_/_/_

324 Name: B:_/_/_ M:_/_/_ D:_/_/_

325 Name: B:_/_/_ M:_/_/_ D:_/_/_

326 Name: B:_/_/_ M:_/_/_ D:_/_/_

327 Name: B:_/_/_ M:_/_/_ D:_/_/_

328 Name: B:_/_/_ M:_/_/_ D:_/_/_

329 Name: B:_/_/_ M:_/_/_ D:_/_/_

330 Name: B:_/_/_ M:_/_/_ D:_/_/_

331 Name: B:_/_/_ M:_/_/_ D:_/_/_

332 Name: B:_/_/_ M:_/_/_ D:_/_/_

333 Name: B:_/_/_ M:_/_/_ D:_/_/_

334 Name: B:_/_/_ M:_/_/_ D:_/_/_

335 Name: B:_/_/_ M:_/_/_ D:_/_/_

336 Name: B:_/_/_ M:_/_/_ D:_/_/_

337 Name: B:_/_/_ M:_/_/_ D:_/_/_

338 Name: B:_/_/_ M:_/_/_ D:_/_/_

339 Name: B:_/_/_ M:_/_/_ D:_/_/_

340 Name: B:_/_/_ M:_/_/_ D:_/_/_

341 Name: B:_/_/_ M:_/_/_ D:_/_/_

342 Name: B:_/_/_ M:_/_/_ D:_/_/_

343 Name: B:_/_/_ M:_/_/_ D:_/_/_

344 Name: B:_/_/_ M:_/_/_ D:_/_/_

345 Name: B:_/_/_ M:_/_/_ D:_/_/_

346 Name: B:_/_/_ M:_/_/_ D:_/_/_

347 Name: B:_/_/_ M:_/_/_ D:_/_/_

348 Name: B:_/_/_ M:_/_/_ D:_/_/_

349 Name: B:_/_/_ M:_/_/_ D:_/_/_

350 Name: B:_/_/_ M:_/_/_ D:_/_/_

351 Name: B:_/_/_ M:_/_/_ D:_/_/_

7X-GREAT-GRANDPARENTS (MALE)		7X-GREAT-GRANDPARENTS (FEMALE)
640 Name: B:_/_/_ M:_/_/_ D:_/_/_	&	641 Name: B:_/_/_ M:_/_/_ D:_/_/_
642 Name: B:_/_/_ M:_/_/_ D:_/_/_	&	643 Name: B:_/_/_ M:_/_/_ D:_/_/_
644 Name: B:_/_/_ M:_/_/_ D:_/_/_	&	645 Name: B:_/_/_ M:_/_/_ D:_/_/_
646 Name: B:_/_/_ M:_/_/_ D:_/_/_	&	647 Name: B:_/_/_ M:_/_/_ D:_/_/_
648 Name: B:_/_/_ M:_/_/_ D:_/_/_	&	649 Name: B:_/_/_ M:_/_/_ D:_/_/_
650 Name: B:_/_/_ M:_/_/_ D:_/_/_	&	651 Name: B:_/_/_ M:_/_/_ D:_/_/_
652 Name: B:_/_/_ M:_/_/_ D:_/_/_	&	653 Name: B:_/_/_ M:_/_/_ D:_/_/_
654 Name: B:_/_/_ M:_/_/_ D:_/_/_	&	655 Name: B:_/_/_ M:_/_/_ D:_/_/_
656 Name: B:_/_/_ M:_/_/_ D:_/_/_	&	657 Name: B:_/_/_ M:_/_/_ D:_/_/_
658 Name: B:_/_/_ M:_/_/_ D:_/_/_	&	659 Name: B:_/_/_ M:_/_/_ D:_/_/_
660 Name: B:_/_/_ M:_/_/_ D:_/_/_	&	661 Name: B:_/_/_ M:_/_/_ D:_/_/_
662 Name: B:_/_/_ M:_/_/_ D:_/_/_	&	663 Name: B:_/_/_ M:_/_/_ D:_/_/_
664 Name: B:_/_/_ M:_/_/_ D:_/_/_	&	665 Name: B:_/_/_ M:_/_/_ D:_/_/_
666 Name: B:_/_/_ M:_/_/_ D:_/_/_	&	667 Name: B:_/_/_ M:_/_/_ D:_/_/_
668 Name: B:_/_/_ M:_/_/_ D:_/_/_	&	669 Name: B:_/_/_ M:_/_/_ D:_/_/_
670 Name: B:_/_/_ M:_/_/_ D:_/_/_	&	671 Name: B:_/_/_ M:_/_/_ D:_/_/_
672 Name: B:_/_/_ M:_/_/_ D:_/_/_	&	673 Name: B:_/_/_ M:_/_/_ D:_/_/_
674 Name: B:_/_/_ M:_/_/_ D:_/_/_	&	675 Name: B:_/_/_ M:_/_/_ D:_/_/_
676 Name: B:_/_/_ M:_/_/_ D:_/_/_	&	677 Name: B:_/_/_ M:_/_/_ D:_/_/_
678 Name: B:_/_/_ M:_/_/_ D:_/_/_	&	679 Name: B:_/_/_ M:_/_/_ D:_/_/_
680 Name: B:_/_/_ M:_/_/_ D:_/_/_	&	681 Name: B:_/_/_ M:_/_/_ D:_/_/_
682 Name: B:_/_/_ M:_/_/_ D:_/_/_	&	683 Name: B:_/_/_ M:_/_/_ D:_/_/_
684 Name: B:_/_/_ M:_/_/_ D:_/_/_	&	685 Name: B:_/_/_ M:_/_/_ D:_/_/_
686 Name: B:_/_/_ M:_/_/_ D:_/_/_	&	687 Name: B:_/_/_ M:_/_/_ D:_/_/_
688 Name: B:_/_/_ M:_/_/_ D:_/_/_	&	689 Name: B:_/_/_ M:_/_/_ D:_/_/_
690 Name: B:_/_/_ M:_/_/_ D:_/_/_	&	691 Name: B:_/_/_ M:_/_/_ D:_/_/_
692 Name: B:_/_/_ M:_/_/_ D:_/_/_	&	693 Name: B:_/_/_ M:_/_/_ D:_/_/_
694 Name: B:_/_/_ M:_/_/_ D:_/_/_	&	695 Name: B:_/_/_ M:_/_/_ D:_/_/_
696 Name: B:_/_/_ M:_/_/_ D:_/_/_	&	697 Name: B:_/_/_ M:_/_/_ D:_/_/_
698 Name: B:_/_/_ M:_/_/_ D:_/_/_	&	699 Name: B:_/_/_ M:_/_/_ D:_/_/_
700 Name: B:_/_/_ M:_/_/_ D:_/_/_	&	701 Name: B:_/_/_ M:_/_/_ D:_/_/_
702 Name: B:_/_/_ M:_/_/_ D:_/_/_	&	703 Name: B:_/_/_ M:_/_/_ D:_/_/_

For previous generations, see previous Family History Record Book

5X-GREAT-GRANDPARENTS

176 Name:
B: / / M: / / D: / /

177 Name:
B: / / M: / / D: / /

178 Name:
B: / / M: / / D: / /

179 Name:
B: / / M: / / D: / /

180 Name:
B: / / M: / / D: / /

181 Name:
B: / / M: / / D: / /

182 Name:
B: / / M: / / D: / /

183 Name:
B: / / M: / / D: / /

184 Name:
B: / / M: / / D: / /

185 Name:
B: / / M: / / D: / /

186 Name:
B: / / M: / / D: / /

187 Name:
B: / / M: / / D: / /

188 Name:
B: / / M: / / D: / /

189 Name:
B: / / M: / / D: / /

190 Name:
B: / / M: / / D: / /

191 Name:
B: / / M: / / D: / /

6X-GREAT-GRANDPARENTS

352 Name: B:_/_/_ M:_/_/_ D:_/_/_

353 Name: B:_/_/_ M:_/_/_ D:_/_/_

354 Name: B:_/_/_ M:_/_/_ D:_/_/_

355 Name: B:_/_/_ M:_/_/_ D:_/_/_

356 Name: B:_/_/_ M:_/_/_ D:_/_/_

357 Name: B:_/_/_ M:_/_/_ D:_/_/_

358 Name: B:_/_/_ M:_/_/_ D:_/_/_

359 Name: B:_/_/_ M:_/_/_ D:_/_/_

360 Name: B:_/_/_ M:_/_/_ D:_/_/_

361 Name: B:_/_/_ M:_/_/_ D:_/_/_

362 Name: B:_/_/_ M:_/_/_ D:_/_/_

363 Name: B:_/_/_ M:_/_/_ D:_/_/_

364 Name: B:_/_/_ M:_/_/_ D:_/_/_

365 Name: B:_/_/_ M:_/_/_ D:_/_/_

366 Name: B:_/_/_ M:_/_/_ D:_/_/_

367 Name: B:_/_/_ M:_/_/_ D:_/_/_

368 Name: B:_/_/_ M:_/_/_ D:_/_/_

369 Name: B:_/_/_ M:_/_/_ D:_/_/_

370 Name: B:_/_/_ M:_/_/_ D:_/_/_

371 Name: B:_/_/_ M:_/_/_ D:_/_/_

372 Name: B:_/_/_ M:_/_/_ D:_/_/_

373 Name: B:_/_/_ M:_/_/_ D:_/_/_

374 Name: B:_/_/_ M:_/_/_ D:_/_/_

375 Name: B:_/_/_ M:_/_/_ D:_/_/_

376 Name: B:_/_/_ M:_/_/_ D:_/_/_

377 Name: B:_/_/_ M:_/_/_ D:_/_/_

378 Name: B:_/_/_ M:_/_/_ D:_/_/_

379 Name: B:_/_/_ M:_/_/_ D:_/_/_

380 Name: B:_/_/_ M:_/_/_ D:_/_/_

381 Name: B:_/_/_ M:_/_/_ D:_/_/_

382 Name: B:_/_/_ M:_/_/_ D:_/_/_

383 Name: B:_/_/_ M:_/_/_ D:_/_/_

7X-GREAT-GRANDPARENTS (MALE)		7X-GREAT-GRANDPARENTS (FEMALE)
704 Name: B:_/_/_ M:_/_/_ D:_/_/_	&	*705* Name: B:_/_/_ M:_/_/_ D:_/_/_
706 Name: B:_/_/_ M:_/_/_ D:_/_/_	&	*707* Name: B:_/_/_ M:_/_/_ D:_/_/_
708 Name: B:_/_/_ M:_/_/_ D:_/_/_	&	*709* Name: B:_/_/_ M:_/_/_ D:_/_/_
710 Name: B:_/_/_ M:_/_/_ D:_/_/_	&	*711* Name: B:_/_/_ M:_/_/_ D:_/_/_
712 Name: B:_/_/_ M:_/_/_ D:_/_/_	&	*713* Name: B:_/_/_ M:_/_/_ D:_/_/_
714 Name: B:_/_/_ M:_/_/_ D:_/_/_	&	*715* Name: B:_/_/_ M:_/_/_ D:_/_/_
716 Name: B:_/_/_ M:_/_/_ D:_/_/_	&	*717* Name: B:_/_/_ M:_/_/_ D:_/_/_
718 Name: B:_/_/_ M:_/_/_ D:_/_/_	&	*719* Name: B:_/_/_ M:_/_/_ D:_/_/_
720 Name: B:_/_/_ M:_/_/_ D:_/_/_	&	*721* Name: B:_/_/_ M:_/_/_ D:_/_/_
722 Name: B:_/_/_ M:_/_/_ D:_/_/_	&	*723* Name: B:_/_/_ M:_/_/_ D:_/_/_
724 Name: B:_/_/_ M:_/_/_ D:_/_/_	&	*725* Name: B:_/_/_ M:_/_/_ D:_/_/_
726 Name: B:_/_/_ M:_/_/_ D:_/_/_	&	*727* Name: B:_/_/_ M:_/_/_ D:_/_/_
728 Name: B:_/_/_ M:_/_/_ D:_/_/_	&	*729* Name: B:_/_/_ M:_/_/_ D:_/_/_
730 Name: B:_/_/_ M:_/_/_ D:_/_/_	&	*731* Name: B:_/_/_ M:_/_/_ D:_/_/_
732 Name: B:_/_/_ M:_/_/_ D:_/_/_	&	*733* Name: B:_/_/_ M:_/_/_ D:_/_/_
734 Name: B:_/_/_ M:_/_/_ D:_/_/_	&	*735* Name: B:_/_/_ M:_/_/_ D:_/_/_
736 Name: B:_/_/_ M:_/_/_ D:_/_/_	&	*737* Name: B:_/_/_ M:_/_/_ D:_/_/_
738 Name: B:_/_/_ M:_/_/_ D:_/_/_	&	*739* Name: B:_/_/_ M:_/_/_ D:_/_/_
740 Name: B:_/_/_ M:_/_/_ D:_/_/_	&	*741* Name: B:_/_/_ M:_/_/_ D:_/_/_
742 Name: B:_/_/_ M:_/_/_ D:_/_/_	&	*743* Name: B:_/_/_ M:_/_/_ D:_/_/_
744 Name: B:_/_/_ M:_/_/_ D:_/_/_	&	*745* Name: B:_/_/_ M:_/_/_ D:_/_/_
746 Name: B:_/_/_ M:_/_/_ D:_/_/_	&	*747* Name: B:_/_/_ M:_/_/_ D:_/_/_
748 Name: B:_/_/_ M:_/_/_ D:_/_/_	&	*749* Name: B:_/_/_ M:_/_/_ D:_/_/_
750 Name: B:_/_/_ M:_/_/_ D:_/_/_	&	*751* Name: B:_/_/_ M:_/_/_ D:_/_/_
752 Name: B:_/_/_ M:_/_/_ D:_/_/_	&	*753* Name: B:_/_/_ M:_/_/_ D:_/_/_
754 Name: B:_/_/_ M:_/_/_ D:_/_/_	&	*755* Name: B:_/_/_ M:_/_/_ D:_/_/_
756 Name: B:_/_/_ M:_/_/_ D:_/_/_	&	*757* Name: B:_/_/_ M:_/_/_ D:_/_/_
758 Name: B:_/_/_ M:_/_/_ D:_/_/_	&	*759* Name: B:_/_/_ M:_/_/_ D:_/_/_
760 Name: B:_/_/_ M:_/_/_ D:_/_/_	&	*761* Name: B:_/_/_ M:_/_/_ D:_/_/_
762 Name: B:_/_/_ M:_/_/_ D:_/_/_	&	*763* Name: B:_/_/_ M:_/_/_ D:_/_/_
764 Name: B:_/_/_ M:_/_/_ D:_/_/_	&	*765* Name: B:_/_/_ M:_/_/_ D:_/_/_
766 Name: B:_/_/_ M:_/_/_ D:_/_/_	&	*767* Name: B:_/_/_ M:_/_/_ D:_/_/_

For previous generations, see previous Family History Record Book

5x-great-grandparents

192 Name:
B: / / M: / / D: / /

193 Name:
B: / / M: / / D: / /

194 Name:
B: / / M: / / D: / /

195 Name:
B: / / M: / / D: / /

196 Name:
B: / / M: / / D: / /

197 Name:
B: / / M: / / D: / /

198 Name:
B: / / M: / / D: / /

199 Name:
B: / / M: / / D: / /

200 Name:
B: / / M: / / D: / /

201 Name:
B: / / M: / / D: / /

202 Name:
B: / / M: / / D: / /

203 Name:
B: / / M: / / D: / /

204 Name:
B: / / M: / / D: / /

205 Name:
B: / / M: / / D: / /

206 Name:
B: / / M: / / D: / /

207 Name:
B: / / M: / / D: / /

6x-great-grandparents

384 Name: B:_/_/_ M:_/_/_ D:_/_/_

385 Name: B:_/_/_ M:_/_/_ D:_/_/_

386 Name: B:_/_/_ M:_/_/_ D:_/_/_

387 Name: B:_/_/_ M:_/_/_ D:_/_/_

388 Name: B:_/_/_ M:_/_/_ D:_/_/_

389 Name: B:_/_/_ M:_/_/_ D:_/_/_

390 Name: B:_/_/_ M:_/_/_ D:_/_/_

391 Name: B:_/_/_ M:_/_/_ D:_/_/_

392 Name: B:_/_/_ M:_/_/_ D:_/_/_

393 Name: B:_/_/_ M:_/_/_ D:_/_/_

394 Name: B:_/_/_ M:_/_/_ D:_/_/_

395 Name: B:_/_/_ M:_/_/_ D:_/_/_

396 Name: B:_/_/_ M:_/_/_ D:_/_/_

397 Name: B:_/_/_ M:_/_/_ D:_/_/_

398 Name: B:_/_/_ M:_/_/_ D:_/_/_

399 Name: B:_/_/_ M:_/_/_ D:_/_/_

400 Name: B:_/_/_ M:_/_/_ D:_/_/_

401 Name: B:_/_/_ M:_/_/_ D:_/_/_

402 Name: B:_/_/_ M:_/_/_ D:_/_/_

403 Name: B:_/_/_ M:_/_/_ D:_/_/_

404 Name: B:_/_/_ M:_/_/_ D:_/_/_

405 Name: B:_/_/_ M:_/_/_ D:_/_/_

406 Name: B:_/_/_ M:_/_/_ D:_/_/_

407 Name: B:_/_/_ M:_/_/_ D:_/_/_

408 Name: B:_/_/_ M:_/_/_ D:_/_/_

409 Name: B:_/_/_ M:_/_/_ D:_/_/_

410 Name: B:_/_/_ M:_/_/_ D:_/_/_

411 Name: B:_/_/_ M:_/_/_ D:_/_/_

412 Name: B:_/_/_ M:_/_/_ D:_/_/_

413 Name: B:_/_/_ M:_/_/_ D:_/_/_

414 Name: B:_/_/_ M:_/_/_ D:_/_/_

415 Name: B:_/_/_ M:_/_/_ D:_/_/_

7X-GREAT-GRANDPARENTS (MALE)		7X-GREAT-GRANDPARENTS (FEMALE)
768 Name: B:_/_/_ M:_/_/_ D:_/_/_	&	**769** Name: B:_/_/_ M:_/_/_ D:_/_/_
770 Name: B:_/_/_ M:_/_/_ D:_/_/_	&	**771** Name: B:_/_/_ M:_/_/_ D:_/_/_
772 Name: B:_/_/_ M:_/_/_ D:_/_/_	&	**773** Name: B:_/_/_ M:_/_/_ D:_/_/_
774 Name: B:_/_/_ M:_/_/_ D:_/_/_	&	**775** Name: B:_/_/_ M:_/_/_ D:_/_/_
776 Name: B:_/_/_ M:_/_/_ D:_/_/_	&	**777** Name: B:_/_/_ M:_/_/_ D:_/_/_
778 Name: B:_/_/_ M:_/_/_ D:_/_/_	&	**779** Name: B:_/_/_ M:_/_/_ D:_/_/_
780 Name: B:_/_/_ M:_/_/_ D:_/_/_	&	**781** Name: B:_/_/_ M:_/_/_ D:_/_/_
782 Name: B:_/_/_ M:_/_/_ D:_/_/_	&	**783** Name: B:_/_/_ M:_/_/_ D:_/_/_
784 Name: B:_/_/_ M:_/_/_ D:_/_/_	&	**785** Name: B:_/_/_ M:_/_/_ D:_/_/_
786 Name: B:_/_/_ M:_/_/_ D:_/_/_	&	**787** Name: B:_/_/_ M:_/_/_ D:_/_/_
788 Name: B:_/_/_ M:_/_/_ D:_/_/_	&	**789** Name: B:_/_/_ M:_/_/_ D:_/_/_
790 Name: B:_/_/_ M:_/_/_ D:_/_/_	&	**791** Name: B:_/_/_ M:_/_/_ D:_/_/_
792 Name: B:_/_/_ M:_/_/_ D:_/_/_	&	**793** Name: B:_/_/_ M:_/_/_ D:_/_/_
794 Name: B:_/_/_ M:_/_/_ D:_/_/_	&	**795** Name: B:_/_/_ M:_/_/_ D:_/_/_
796 Name: B:_/_/_ M:_/_/_ D:_/_/_	&	**797** Name: B:_/_/_ M:_/_/_ D:_/_/_
798 Name: B:_/_/_ M:_/_/_ D:_/_/_	&	**799** Name: B:_/_/_ M:_/_/_ D:_/_/_
800 Name: B:_/_/_ M:_/_/_ D:_/_/_	&	**801** Name: B:_/_/_ M:_/_/_ D:_/_/_
802 Name: B:_/_/_ M:_/_/_ D:_/_/_	&	**803** Name: B:_/_/_ M:_/_/_ D:_/_/_
804 Name: B:_/_/_ M:_/_/_ D:_/_/_	&	**805** Name: B:_/_/_ M:_/_/_ D:_/_/_
806 Name: B:_/_/_ M:_/_/_ D:_/_/_	&	**807** Name: B:_/_/_ M:_/_/_ D:_/_/_
808 Name: B:_/_/_ M:_/_/_ D:_/_/_	&	**809** Name: B:_/_/_ M:_/_/_ D:_/_/_
810 Name: B:_/_/_ M:_/_/_ D:_/_/_	&	**811** Name: B:_/_/_ M:_/_/_ D:_/_/_
812 Name: B:_/_/_ M:_/_/_ D:_/_/_	&	**813** Name: B:_/_/_ M:_/_/_ D:_/_/_
814 Name: B:_/_/_ M:_/_/_ D:_/_/_	&	**815** Name: B:_/_/_ M:_/_/_ D:_/_/_
816 Name: B:_/_/_ M:_/_/_ D:_/_/_	&	**817** Name: B:_/_/_ M:_/_/_ D:_/_/_
818 Name: B:_/_/_ M:_/_/_ D:_/_/_	&	**819** Name: B:_/_/_ M:_/_/_ D:_/_/_
820 Name: B:_/_/_ M:_/_/_ D:_/_/_	&	**821** Name: B:_/_/_ M:_/_/_ D:_/_/_
822 Name: B:_/_/_ M:_/_/_ D:_/_/_	&	**823** Name: B:_/_/_ M:_/_/_ D:_/_/_
824 Name: B:_/_/_ M:_/_/_ D:_/_/_	&	**825** Name: B:_/_/_ M:_/_/_ D:_/_/_
826 Name: B:_/_/_ M:_/_/_ D:_/_/_	&	**827** Name: B:_/_/_ M:_/_/_ D:_/_/_
828 Name: B:_/_/_ M:_/_/_ D:_/_/_	&	**829** Name: B:_/_/_ M:_/_/_ D:_/_/_
830 Name: B:_/_/_ M:_/_/_ D:_/_/_	&	**831** Name: B:_/_/_ M:_/_/_ D:_/_/_

FOR PREVIOUS GENERATIONS, SEE PREVIOUS FAMILY HISTORY RECORD BOOK

5X-GREAT-GRANDPARENTS

208 Name:
B: / / M: / / D: / /

209 Name:
B: / / M: / / D: / /

210 Name:
B: / / M: / / D: / /

211 Name:
B: / / M: / / D: / /

212 Name:
B: / / M: / / D: / /

213 Name:
B: / / M: / / D: / /

214 Name:
B: / / M: / / D: / /

215 Name:
B: / / M: / / D: / /

216 Name:
B: / / M: / / D: / /

217 Name:
B: / / M: / / D: / /

218 Name:
B: / / M: / / D: / /

219 Name:
B: / / M: / / D: / /

220 Name:
B: / / M: / / D: / /

221 Name:
B: / / M: / / D: / /

222 Name:
B: / / M: / / D: / /

223 Name:
B: / / M: / / D: / /

6X-GREAT-GRANDPARENTS

416 Name: B:_/_/_ M:_/_/_ D:_/_/_

417 Name: B:_/_/_ M:_/_/_ D:_/_/_

418 Name: B:_/_/_ M:_/_/_ D:_/_/_

419 Name: B:_/_/_ M:_/_/_ D:_/_/_

420 Name: B:_/_/_ M:_/_/_ D:_/_/_

421 Name: B:_/_/_ M:_/_/_ D:_/_/_

422 Name: B:_/_/_ M:_/_/_ D:_/_/_

423 Name: B:_/_/_ M:_/_/_ D:_/_/_

424 Name: B:_/_/_ M:_/_/_ D:_/_/_

425 Name: B:_/_/_ M:_/_/_ D:_/_/_

426 Name: B:_/_/_ M:_/_/_ D:_/_/_

427 Name: B:_/_/_ M:_/_/_ D:_/_/_

428 Name: B:_/_/_ M:_/_/_ D:_/_/_

429 Name: B:_/_/_ M:_/_/_ D:_/_/_

430 Name: B:_/_/_ M:_/_/_ D:_/_/_

431 Name: B:_/_/_ M:_/_/_ D:_/_/_

432 Name: B:_/_/_ M:_/_/_ D:_/_/_

433 Name: B:_/_/_ M:_/_/_ D:_/_/_

434 Name: B:_/_/_ M:_/_/_ D:_/_/_

435 Name: B:_/_/_ M:_/_/_ D:_/_/_

436 Name: B:_/_/_ M:_/_/_ D:_/_/_

437 Name: B:_/_/_ M:_/_/_ D:_/_/_

438 Name: B:_/_/_ M:_/_/_ D:_/_/_

439 Name: B:_/_/_ M:_/_/_ D:_/_/_

440 Name: B:_/_/_ M:_/_/_ D:_/_/_

441 Name: B:_/_/_ M:_/_/_ D:_/_/_

442 Name: B:_/_/_ M:_/_/_ D:_/_/_

443 Name: B:_/_/_ M:_/_/_ D:_/_/_

444 Name: B:_/_/_ M:_/_/_ D:_/_/_

445 Name: B:_/_/_ M:_/_/_ D:_/_/_

446 Name: B:_/_/_ M:_/_/_ D:_/_/_

447 Name: B:_/_/_ M:_/_/_ D:_/_/_

7X-GREAT-GRANDPARENTS (MALE)		7X-GREAT-GRANDPARENTS (FEMALE)
832 Name: B:_/_/_ M:_/_/_ D:_/_/_	&	*833* Name: B:_/_/_ M:_/_/_ D:_/_/_
834 Name: B:_/_/_ M:_/_/_ D:_/_/_	&	*835* Name: B:_/_/_ M:_/_/_ D:_/_/_
836 Name: B:_/_/_ M:_/_/_ D:_/_/_	&	*837* Name: B:_/_/_ M:_/_/_ D:_/_/_
838 Name: B:_/_/_ M:_/_/_ D:_/_/_	&	*839* Name: B:_/_/_ M:_/_/_ D:_/_/_
840 Name: B:_/_/_ M:_/_/_ D:_/_/_	&	*841* Name: B:_/_/_ M:_/_/_ D:_/_/_
842 Name: B:_/_/_ M:_/_/_ D:_/_/_	&	*843* Name: B:_/_/_ M:_/_/_ D:_/_/_
844 Name: B:_/_/_ M:_/_/_ D:_/_/_	&	*845* Name: B:_/_/_ M:_/_/_ D:_/_/_
846 Name: B:_/_/_ M:_/_/_ D:_/_/_	&	*847* Name: B:_/_/_ M:_/_/_ D:_/_/_
848 Name: B:_/_/_ M:_/_/_ D:_/_/_	&	*849* Name: B:_/_/_ M:_/_/_ D:_/_/_
850 Name: B:_/_/_ M:_/_/_ D:_/_/_	&	*851* Name: B:_/_/_ M:_/_/_ D:_/_/_
852 Name: B:_/_/_ M:_/_/_ D:_/_/_	&	*853* Name: B:_/_/_ M:_/_/_ D:_/_/_
854 Name: B:_/_/_ M:_/_/_ D:_/_/_	&	*855* Name: B:_/_/_ M:_/_/_ D:_/_/_
856 Name: B:_/_/_ M:_/_/_ D:_/_/_	&	*857* Name: B:_/_/_ M:_/_/_ D:_/_/_
858 Name: B:_/_/_ M:_/_/_ D:_/_/_	&	*859* Name: B:_/_/_ M:_/_/_ D:_/_/_
860 Name: B:_/_/_ M:_/_/_ D:_/_/_	&	*861* Name: B:_/_/_ M:_/_/_ D:_/_/_
862 Name: B:_/_/_ M:_/_/_ D:_/_/_	&	*863* Name: B:_/_/_ M:_/_/_ D:_/_/_
864 Name: B:_/_/_ M:_/_/_ D:_/_/_	&	*865* Name: B:_/_/_ M:_/_/_ D:_/_/_
866 Name: B:_/_/_ M:_/_/_ D:_/_/_	&	*867* Name: B:_/_/_ M:_/_/_ D:_/_/_
868 Name: B:_/_/_ M:_/_/_ D:_/_/_	&	*869* Name: B:_/_/_ M:_/_/_ D:_/_/_
870 Name: B:_/_/_ M:_/_/_ D:_/_/_	&	*871* Name: B:_/_/_ M:_/_/_ D:_/_/_
872 Name: B:_/_/_ M:_/_/_ D:_/_/_	&	*873* Name: B:_/_/_ M:_/_/_ D:_/_/_
874 Name: B:_/_/_ M:_/_/_ D:_/_/_	&	*875* Name: B:_/_/_ M:_/_/_ D:_/_/_
876 Name: B:_/_/_ M:_/_/_ D:_/_/_	&	*877* Name: B:_/_/_ M:_/_/_ D:_/_/_
878 Name: B:_/_/_ M:_/_/_ D:_/_/_	&	*879* Name: B:_/_/_ M:_/_/_ D:_/_/_
880 Name: B:_/_/_ M:_/_/_ D:_/_/_	&	*881* Name: B:_/_/_ M:_/_/_ D:_/_/_
882 Name: B:_/_/_ M:_/_/_ D:_/_/_	&	*883* Name: B:_/_/_ M:_/_/_ D:_/_/_
884 Name: B:_/_/_ M:_/_/_ D:_/_/_	&	*885* Name: B:_/_/_ M:_/_/_ D:_/_/_
886 Name: B:_/_/_ M:_/_/_ D:_/_/_	&	*887* Name: B:_/_/_ M:_/_/_ D:_/_/_
888 Name: B:_/_/_ M:_/_/_ D:_/_/_	&	*889* Name: B:_/_/_ M:_/_/_ D:_/_/_
890 Name: B:_/_/_ M:_/_/_ D:_/_/_	&	*891* Name: B:_/_/_ M:_/_/_ D:_/_/_
892 Name: B:_/_/_ M:_/_/_ D:_/_/_	&	*893* Name: B:_/_/_ M:_/_/_ D:_/_/_
894 Name: B:_/_/_ M:_/_/_ D:_/_/_	&	*895* Name: B:_/_/_ M:_/_/_ D:_/_/_

5X-GREAT-GRANDPARENTS

224 Name:
B: / / M: / / D: / /

225 Name:
B: / / M: / / D: / /

226 Name:
B: / / M: / / D: / /

227 Name:
B: / / M: / / D: / /

228 Name:
B: / / M: / / D: / /

229 Name:
B: / / M: / / D: / /

230 Name:
B: / / M: / / D: / /

231 Name:
B: / / M: / / D: / /

232 Name:
B: / / M: / / D: / /

233 Name:
B: / / M: / / D: / /

234 Name:
B: / / M: / / D: / /

235 Name:
B: / / M: / / D: / /

236 Name:
B: / / M: / / D: / /

237 Name:
B: / / M: / / D: / /

238 Name:
B: / / M: / / D: / /

239 Name:
B: / / M: / / D: / /

6X-GREAT-GRANDPARENTS

448 Name: B:_/_/_ M:_/_/_ D:_/_/_

449 Name: B:_/_/_ M:_/_/_ D:_/_/_

450 Name: B:_/_/_ M:_/_/_ D:_/_/_

451 Name: B:_/_/_ M:_/_/_ D:_/_/_

452 Name: B:_/_/_ M:_/_/_ D:_/_/_

453 Name: B:_/_/_ M:_/_/_ D:_/_/_

454 Name: B:_/_/_ M:_/_/_ D:_/_/_

455 Name: B:_/_/_ M:_/_/_ D:_/_/_

456 Name: B:_/_/_ M:_/_/_ D:_/_/_

457 Name: B:_/_/_ M:_/_/_ D:_/_/_

458 Name: B:_/_/_ M:_/_/_ D:_/_/_

459 Name: B:_/_/_ M:_/_/_ D:_/_/_

460 Name: B:_/_/_ M:_/_/_ D:_/_/_

461 Name: B:_/_/_ M:_/_/_ D:_/_/_

462 Name: B:_/_/_ M:_/_/_ D:_/_/_

463 Name: B:_/_/_ M:_/_/_ D:_/_/_

464 Name: B:_/_/_ M:_/_/_ D:_/_/_

465 Name: B:_/_/_ M:_/_/_ D:_/_/_

466 Name: B:_/_/_ M:_/_/_ D:_/_/_

467 Name: B:_/_/_ M:_/_/_ D:_/_/_

468 Name: B:_/_/_ M:_/_/_ D:_/_/_

469 Name: B:_/_/_ M:_/_/_ D:_/_/_

470 Name: B:_/_/_ M:_/_/_ D:_/_/_

471 Name: B:_/_/_ M:_/_/_ D:_/_/_

472 Name: B:_/_/_ M:_/_/_ D:_/_/_

473 Name: B:_/_/_ M:_/_/_ D:_/_/_

474 Name: B:_/_/_ M:_/_/_ D:_/_/_

475 Name: B:_/_/_ M:_/_/_ D:_/_/_

476 Name: B:_/_/_ M:_/_/_ D:_/_/_

477 Name: B:_/_/_ M:_/_/_ D:_/_/_

478 Name: B:_/_/_ M:_/_/_ D:_/_/_

479 Name: B:_/_/_ M:_/_/_ D:_/_/_

FOR PREVIOUS GENERATIONS, SEE PREVIOUS FAMILY HISTORY RECORD BOOK

7X-GREAT-GRANDPARENTS (MALE)		7X-GREAT-GRANDPARENTS (FEMALE)
896 Name: B:_/_/_ M:_/_/_ D:_/_/_	&	**897** Name: B:_/_/_ M:_/_/_ D:_/_/_
898 Name: B:_/_/_ M:_/_/_ D:_/_/_	&	**899** Name: B:_/_/_ M:_/_/_ D:_/_/_
900 Name: B:_/_/_ M:_/_/_ D:_/_/_	&	**901** Name: B:_/_/_ M:_/_/_ D:_/_/_
902 Name: B:_/_/_ M:_/_/_ D:_/_/_	&	**903** Name: B:_/_/_ M:_/_/_ D:_/_/_
904 Name: B:_/_/_ M:_/_/_ D:_/_/_	&	**905** Name: B:_/_/_ M:_/_/_ D:_/_/_
906 Name: B:_/_/_ M:_/_/_ D:_/_/_	&	**907** Name: B:_/_/_ M:_/_/_ D:_/_/_
908 Name: B:_/_/_ M:_/_/_ D:_/_/_	&	**909** Name: B:_/_/_ M:_/_/_ D:_/_/_
910 Name: B:_/_/_ M:_/_/_ D:_/_/_	&	**911** Name: B:_/_/_ M:_/_/_ D:_/_/_
912 Name: B:_/_/_ M:_/_/_ D:_/_/_	&	**913** Name: B:_/_/_ M:_/_/_ D:_/_/_
914 Name: B:_/_/_ M:_/_/_ D:_/_/_	&	**915** Name: B:_/_/_ M:_/_/_ D:_/_/_
916 Name: B:_/_/_ M:_/_/_ D:_/_/_	&	**917** Name: B:_/_/_ M:_/_/_ D:_/_/_
918 Name: B:_/_/_ M:_/_/_ D:_/_/_	&	**919** Name: B:_/_/_ M:_/_/_ D:_/_/_
920 Name: B:_/_/_ M:_/_/_ D:_/_/_	&	**921** Name: B:_/_/_ M:_/_/_ D:_/_/_
922 Name: B:_/_/_ M:_/_/_ D:_/_/_	&	**923** Name: B:_/_/_ M:_/_/_ D:_/_/_
924 Name: B:_/_/_ M:_/_/_ D:_/_/_	&	**925** Name: B:_/_/_ M:_/_/_ D:_/_/_
926 Name: B:_/_/_ M:_/_/_ D:_/_/_	&	**927** Name: B:_/_/_ M:_/_/_ D:_/_/_
928 Name: B:_/_/_ M:_/_/_ D:_/_/_	&	**929** Name: B:_/_/_ M:_/_/_ D:_/_/_
930 Name: B:_/_/_ M:_/_/_ D:_/_/_	&	**931** Name: B:_/_/_ M:_/_/_ D:_/_/_
932 Name: B:_/_/_ M:_/_/_ D:_/_/_	&	**933** Name: B:_/_/_ M:_/_/_ D:_/_/_
934 Name: B:_/_/_ M:_/_/_ D:_/_/_	&	**935** Name: B:_/_/_ M:_/_/_ D:_/_/_
936 Name: B:_/_/_ M:_/_/_ D:_/_/_	&	**937** Name: B:_/_/_ M:_/_/_ D:_/_/_
938 Name: B:_/_/_ M:_/_/_ D:_/_/_	&	**939** Name: B:_/_/_ M:_/_/_ D:_/_/_
940 Name: B:_/_/_ M:_/_/_ D:_/_/_	&	**941** Name: B:_/_/_ M:_/_/_ D:_/_/_
942 Name: B:_/_/_ M:_/_/_ D:_/_/_	&	**943** Name: B:_/_/_ M:_/_/_ D:_/_/_
944 Name: B:_/_/_ M:_/_/_ D:_/_/_	&	**945** Name: B:_/_/_ M:_/_/_ D:_/_/_
946 Name: B:_/_/_ M:_/_/_ D:_/_/_	&	**947** Name: B:_/_/_ M:_/_/_ D:_/_/_
948 Name: B:_/_/_ M:_/_/_ D:_/_/_	&	**949** Name: B:_/_/_ M:_/_/_ D:_/_/_
950 Name: B:_/_/_ M:_/_/_ D:_/_/_	&	**951** Name: B:_/_/_ M:_/_/_ D:_/_/_
952 Name: B:_/_/_ M:_/_/_ D:_/_/_	&	**953** Name: B:_/_/_ M:_/_/_ D:_/_/_
954 Name: B:_/_/_ M:_/_/_ D:_/_/_	&	**955** Name: B:_/_/_ M:_/_/_ D:_/_/_
956 Name: B:_/_/_ M:_/_/_ D:_/_/_	&	**957** Name: B:_/_/_ M:_/_/_ D:_/_/_
958 Name: B:_/_/_ M:_/_/_ D:_/_/_	&	**959** Name: B:_/_/_ M:_/_/_ D:_/_/_

5X-GREAT-GRANDPARENTS

240 Name:
B: / / M: / / D: / /

241 Name:
B: / / M: / / D: / /

242 Name:
B: / / M: / / D: / /

243 Name:
B: / / M: / / D: / /

244 Name:
B: / / M: / / D: / /

245 Name:
B: / / M: / / D: / /

246 Name:
B: / / M: / / D: / /

247 Name:
B: / / M: / / D: / /

248 Name:
B: / / M: / / D: / /

249 Name:
B: / / M: / / D: / /

250 Name:
B: / / M: / / D: / /

251 Name:
B: / / M: / / D: / /

252 Name:
B: / / M: / / D: / /

253 Name:
B: / / M: / / D: / /

254 Name:
B: / / M: / / D: / /

255 Name:
B: / / M: / / D: / /

6X-GREAT-GRANDPARENTS

480 Name: B:_/_/_ M:_/_/_ D:_/_/_

481 Name: B:_/_/_ M:_/_/_ D:_/_/_

482 Name: B:_/_/_ M:_/_/_ D:_/_/_

483 Name: B:_/_/_ M:_/_/_ D:_/_/_

484 Name: B:_/_/_ M:_/_/_ D:_/_/_

485 Name: B:_/_/_ M:_/_/_ D:_/_/_

486 Name: B:_/_/_ M:_/_/_ D:_/_/_

487 Name: B:_/_/_ M:_/_/_ D:_/_/_

488 Name: B:_/_/_ M:_/_/_ D:_/_/_

489 Name: B:_/_/_ M:_/_/_ D:_/_/_

490 Name: B:_/_/_ M:_/_/_ D:_/_/_

491 Name: B:_/_/_ M:_/_/_ D:_/_/_

492 Name: B:_/_/_ M:_/_/_ D:_/_/_

493 Name: B:_/_/_ M:_/_/_ D:_/_/_

494 Name: B:_/_/_ M:_/_/_ D:_/_/_

495 Name: B:_/_/_ M:_/_/_ D:_/_/_

496 Name: B:_/_/_ M:_/_/_ D:_/_/_

497 Name: B:_/_/_ M:_/_/_ D:_/_/_

498 Name: B:_/_/_ M:_/_/_ D:_/_/_

499 Name: B:_/_/_ M:_/_/_ D:_/_/_

500 Name: B:_/_/_ M:_/_/_ D:_/_/_

501 Name: B:_/_/_ M:_/_/_ D:_/_/_

502 Name: B:_/_/_ M:_/_/_ D:_/_/_

503 Name: B:_/_/_ M:_/_/_ D:_/_/_

504 Name: B:_/_/_ M:_/_/_ D:_/_/_

505 Name: B:_/_/_ M:_/_/_ D:_/_/_

506 Name: B:_/_/_ M:_/_/_ D:_/_/_

507 Name: B:_/_/_ M:_/_/_ D:_/_/_

508 Name: B:_/_/_ M:_/_/_ D:_/_/_

509 Name: B:_/_/_ M:_/_/_ D:_/_/_

510 Name: B:_/_/_ M:_/_/_ D:_/_/_

511 Name: B:_/_/_ M:_/_/_ D:_/_/_

For previous generations, see previous Family History Record Book

7X-GREAT-GRANDPARENTS (MALE)		7X-GREAT-GRANDPARENTS (FEMALE)
960 Name: B:_/_/_ M:_/_/_ D:_/_/_	&	**961** Name: B:_/_/_ M:_/_/_ D:_/_/_
962 Name: B:_/_/_ M:_/_/_ D:_/_/_	&	**963** Name: B:_/_/_ M:_/_/_ D:_/_/_
964 Name: B:_/_/_ M:_/_/_ D:_/_/_	&	**965** Name: B:_/_/_ M:_/_/_ D:_/_/_
966 Name: B:_/_/_ M:_/_/_ D:_/_/_	&	**967** Name: B:_/_/_ M:_/_/_ D:_/_/_
968 Name: B:_/_/_ M:_/_/_ D:_/_/_	&	**969** Name: B:_/_/_ M:_/_/_ D:_/_/_
970 Name: B:_/_/_ M:_/_/_ D:_/_/_	&	**971** Name: B:_/_/_ M:_/_/_ D:_/_/_
972 Name: B:_/_/_ M:_/_/_ D:_/_/_	&	**973** Name: B:_/_/_ M:_/_/_ D:_/_/_
974 Name: B:_/_/_ M:_/_/_ D:_/_/_	&	**975** Name: B:_/_/_ M:_/_/_ D:_/_/_
976 Name: B:_/_/_ M:_/_/_ D:_/_/_	&	**977** Name: B:_/_/_ M:_/_/_ D:_/_/_
978 Name: B:_/_/_ M:_/_/_ D:_/_/_	&	**979** Name: B:_/_/_ M:_/_/_ D:_/_/_
980 Name: B:_/_/_ M:_/_/_ D:_/_/_	&	**981** Name: B:_/_/_ M:_/_/_ D:_/_/_
982 Name: B:_/_/_ M:_/_/_ D:_/_/_	&	**983** Name: B:_/_/_ M:_/_/_ D:_/_/_
984 Name: B:_/_/_ M:_/_/_ D:_/_/_	&	**985** Name: B:_/_/_ M:_/_/_ D:_/_/_
986 Name: B:_/_/_ M:_/_/_ D:_/_/_	&	**987** Name: B:_/_/_ M:_/_/_ D:_/_/_
988 Name: B:_/_/_ M:_/_/_ D:_/_/_	&	**989** Name: B:_/_/_ M:_/_/_ D:_/_/_
990 Name: B:_/_/_ M:_/_/_ D:_/_/_	&	**991** Name: B:_/_/_ M:_/_/_ D:_/_/_
992 Name: B:_/_/_ M:_/_/_ D:_/_/_	&	**993** Name: B:_/_/_ M:_/_/_ D:_/_/_
994 Name: B:_/_/_ M:_/_/_ D:_/_/_	&	**995** Name: B:_/_/_ M:_/_/_ D:_/_/_
996 Name: B:_/_/_ M:_/_/_ D:_/_/_	&	**997** Name: B:_/_/_ M:_/_/_ D:_/_/_
998 Name: B:_/_/_ M:_/_/_ D:_/_/_	&	**999** Name: B:_/_/_ M:_/_/_ D:_/_/_
1000 Name: B:_/_/_ M:_/_/_ D:_/_/_	&	**1001** Name: B:_/_/_ M:_/_/_ D:_/_/_
1002 Name: B:_/_/_ M:_/_/_ D:_/_/_	&	**1003** Name: B:_/_/_ M:_/_/_ D:_/_/_
1004 Name: B:_/_/_ M:_/_/_ D:_/_/_	&	**1005** Name: B:_/_/_ M:_/_/_ D:_/_/_
1006 Name: B:_/_/_ M:_/_/_ D:_/_/_	&	**1007** Name: B:_/_/_ M:_/_/_ D:_/_/_
1008 Name: B:_/_/_ M:_/_/_ D:_/_/_	&	**1009** Name: B:_/_/_ M:_/_/_ D:_/_/_
1010 Name: B:_/_/_ M:_/_/_ D:_/_/_	&	**1011** Name: B:_/_/_ M:_/_/_ D:_/_/_
1012 Name: B:_/_/_ M:_/_/_ D:_/_/_	&	**1013** Name: B:_/_/_ M:_/_/_ D:_/_/_
1014 Name: B:_/_/_ M:_/_/_ D:_/_/_	&	**1015** Name: B:_/_/_ M:_/_/_ D:_/_/_
1016 Name: B:_/_/_ M:_/_/_ D:_/_/_	&	**1017** Name: B:_/_/_ M:_/_/_ D:_/_/_
1018 Name: B:_/_/_ M:_/_/_ D:_/_/_	&	**1019** Name: B:_/_/_ M:_/_/_ D:_/_/_
1020 Name: B:_/_/_ M:_/_/_ D:_/_/_	&	**1021** Name: B:_/_/_ M:_/_/_ D:_/_/_
1022 Name: B:_/_/_ M:_/_/_ D:_/_/_	&	**1023** Name: B:_/_/_ M:_/_/_ D:_/_/_

256 Name 6x-Great-Grandfather

DATE	SOURCE	INFORMATION
/ /		Birth
/ /		Baptism
/ /		
/ /		
/ /		
/ /		
/ /		
/ /		
/ /		
/ /		
/ /		
/ /		
/ /		
/ /		
/ /		Death
/ /		Burial

...the child of...

512 Name 7x-Great-Grandfather

DATE	SOURCE	INFORMATION
/ /		Birth
/ /		Baptism
/ /		
/ /		
/ /		
/ /		
/ /		
/ /		
/ /		
/ /		
/ /		Death
/ /		Burial

513 Name 7x-Great-Grandmother

DATE	SOURCE	INFORMATION
/ /		Birth
/ /		Baptism
/ /		
/ /		
/ /		
/ /		
/ /		
/ /		
/ /		
/ /		
/ /		Death
/ /		Burial

Name 257

DATE	SOURCE	INFORMATION
/ /		Birth
/ /		Baptism
/ /		
/ /		
/ /		
/ /		
/ /		
/ /		
/ /		
/ /		
/ /		
/ /		
/ /		
/ /		
/ /		Death
/ /		Burial

...the child of...

514 **Name** 7x-Great-Grandfather

DATE	SOURCE	INFORMATION
/ /		Birth
/ /		Baptism
/ /		
/ /		
/ /		
/ /		
/ /		
/ /		
/ /		
/ /		
/ /		Death
/ /		Burial

515 **Name** 7x-Great-Grandmother

DATE	SOURCE	INFORMATION
/ /		Birth
/ /		Baptism
/ /		
/ /		
/ /		
/ /		
/ /		
/ /		
/ /		
/ /		
/ /		Death
/ /		Burial

258 Name

6x-GREAT-GRANDFATHER

DATE	SOURCE	INFORMATION
/ /		Birth
/ /		Baptism
/ /		
/ /		
/ /		
/ /		
/ /		
/ /		
/ /		
/ /		
/ /		
/ /		
/ /		
/ /		
/ /		Death
/ /		Burial

...the child of...

516 Name

7x-GREAT-GRANDFATHER

DATE	SOURCE	INFORMATION
/ /		Birth
/ /		Baptism
/ /		
/ /		
/ /		
/ /		
/ /		
/ /		
/ /		
/ /		
/ /		Death
/ /		Burial

517 Name

7x-GREAT-GRANDMOTHER

DATE	SOURCE	INFORMATION
/ /		Birth
/ /		Baptism
/ /		
/ /		
/ /		
/ /		
/ /		
/ /		
/ /		
/ /		
/ /		Death
/ /		Burial

Name 259

DATE	SOURCE	INFORMATION
/ /		Birth
/ /		Baptism
/ /		
/ /		
/ /		
/ /		
/ /		
/ /		
/ /		
/ /		
/ /		
/ /		
/ /		
/ /		
/ /		Death
/ /		Burial

...the child of...

518 **Name** 7x-Great-Grandfather

DATE	SOURCE	INFORMATION
/ /		Birth
/ /		Baptism
/ /		
/ /		
/ /		
/ /		
/ /		
/ /		
/ /		
/ /		
/ /		Death
/ /		Burial

519 **Name** 7x-Great-Grandmother

DATE	SOURCE	INFORMATION
/ /		Birth
/ /		Baptism
/ /		
/ /		
/ /		
/ /		
/ /		
/ /		
/ /		
/ /		
/ /		Death
/ /		Burial

260 Name

6x-Great-Grandfather

DATE	SOURCE	INFORMATION
/ /		Birth
/ /		Baptism
/ /		
/ /		
/ /		
/ /		
/ /		
/ /		
/ /		
/ /		
/ /		
/ /		
/ /		
/ /		
/ /		Death
/ /		Burial

...the child of...

520 Name

7x-Great-Grandfather

DATE	SOURCE	INFORMATION
/ /		Birth
/ /		Baptism
/ /		
/ /		
/ /		
/ /		
/ /		
/ /		
/ /		
/ /		
/ /		Death
/ /		Burial

521 Name

7x-Great-Grandmother

DATE	SOURCE	INFORMATION
/ /		Birth
/ /		Baptism
/ /		
/ /		
/ /		
/ /		
/ /		
/ /		
/ /		
/ /		
/ /		Death
/ /		Burial

Name 261

DATE	SOURCE	INFORMATION
/ /		Birth
/ /		Baptism
/ /		
/ /		
/ /		
/ /		
/ /		
/ /		
/ /		
/ /		
/ /		
/ /		
/ /		
/ /		
/ /		Death
/ /		Burial

...the child of...

522 **Name** 7x-Great-Grandfather

DATE	SOURCE	INFORMATION
/ /		Birth
/ /		Baptism
/ /		
/ /		
/ /		
/ /		
/ /		
/ /		
/ /		
/ /		
/ /		Death
/ /		Burial

523 **Name** 7x-Great-Grandmother

DATE	SOURCE	INFORMATION
/ /		Birth
/ /		Baptism
/ /		
/ /		
/ /		
/ /		
/ /		
/ /		
/ /		
/ /		
/ /		Death
/ /		Burial

262 Name

6x-Great-Grandfather

DATE	SOURCE	INFORMATION
/ /		Birth
/ /		Baptism
/ /		
/ /		
/ /		
/ /		
/ /		
/ /		
/ /		
/ /		
/ /		
/ /		
/ /		
/ /		
/ /		Death
/ /		Burial

...the child of...

524 Name

7x-Great-Grandfather

DATE	SOURCE	INFORMATION
/ /		Birth
/ /		Baptism
/ /		
/ /		
/ /		
/ /		
/ /		
/ /		
/ /		
/ /		
/ /		Death
/ /		Burial

525 Name

7x-Great-Grandmother

DATE	SOURCE	INFORMATION
/ /		Birth
/ /		Baptism
/ /		
/ /		
/ /		
/ /		
/ /		
/ /		
/ /		
/ /		
/ /		Death
/ /		Burial

Name **263**

DATE	SOURCE	INFORMATION
/ /		Birth
/ /		Baptism
/ /		
/ /		
/ /		
/ /		
/ /		
/ /		
/ /		
/ /		
/ /		
/ /		
/ /		
/ /		
/ /		Death
/ /		Burial

...the child of...

526 Name 7x-Great-Grandfather

DATE	SOURCE	INFORMATION
/ /		Birth
/ /		Baptism
/ /		
/ /		
/ /		
/ /		
/ /		
/ /		
/ /		
/ /		
/ /		Death
/ /		Burial

527 Name 7x-Great-Grandmother

DATE	SOURCE	INFORMATION
/ /		Birth
/ /		Baptism
/ /		
/ /		
/ /		
/ /		
/ /		
/ /		
/ /		
/ /		
/ /		Death
/ /		Burial

264 Name

6x-Great-Grandfather

DATE	SOURCE	INFORMATION
/ /		Birth
/ /		Baptism
/ /		
/ /		
/ /		
/ /		
/ /		
/ /		
/ /		
/ /		
/ /		
/ /		
/ /		
/ /		
/ /		Death
/ /		Burial

...the child of...

528 Name

7x-Great-Grandfather

DATE	SOURCE	INFORMATION
/ /		Birth
/ /		Baptism
/ /		
/ /		
/ /		
/ /		
/ /		
/ /		
/ /		
/ /		
/ /		Death
/ /		Burial

529 Name

7x-Great-Grandmother

DATE	SOURCE	INFORMATION
/ /		Birth
/ /		Baptism
/ /		
/ /		
/ /		
/ /		
/ /		
/ /		
/ /		
/ /		
/ /		Death
/ /		Burial

Name 265

DATE	SOURCE	INFORMATION
/ /		Birth
/ /		Baptism
/ /		
/ /		
/ /		
/ /		
/ /		
/ /		
/ /		
/ /		
/ /		
/ /		
/ /		
/ /		
/ /		Death
/ /		Burial

...the child of...

530 **Name** 7x-Great-Grandfather

DATE	SOURCE	INFORMATION
/ /		Birth
/ /		Baptism
/ /		
/ /		
/ /		
/ /		
/ /		
/ /		
/ /		
/ /		
/ /		Death
/ /		Burial

531 **Name** 7x-Great-Grandmother

DATE	SOURCE	INFORMATION
/ /		Birth
/ /		Baptism
/ /		
/ /		
/ /		
/ /		
/ /		
/ /		
/ /		
/ /		
/ /		Death
/ /		Burial

266 Name

6x-Great-Grandfather

DATE	SOURCE	INFORMATION
/ /		Birth
/ /		Baptism
/ /		
/ /		
/ /		
/ /		
/ /		
/ /		
/ /		
/ /		
/ /		
/ /		
/ /		
/ /		
/ /		Death
/ /		Burial

...the child of...

532 Name

7x-Great-Grandfather

DATE	SOURCE	INFORMATION
/ /		Birth
/ /		Baptism
/ /		
/ /		
/ /		
/ /		
/ /		
/ /		
/ /		
/ /		
/ /		Death
/ /		Burial

533 Name

7x-Great-Grandmother

DATE	SOURCE	INFORMATION
/ /		Birth
/ /		Baptism
/ /		
/ /		
/ /		
/ /		
/ /		
/ /		
/ /		
/ /		
/ /		Death
/ /		Burial

6x-Great-Grandmother

Name 267

DATE	SOURCE	INFORMATION
/ /		Birth
/ /		Baptism
/ /		
/ /		
/ /		
/ /		
/ /		
/ /		
/ /		
/ /		
/ /		
/ /		
/ /		
/ /		
/ /		Death
/ /		Burial

...the child of...

534 Name 7x-Great-Grandfather

DATE	SOURCE	INFORMATION
/ /		Birth
/ /		Baptism
/ /		
/ /		
/ /		
/ /		
/ /		
/ /		
/ /		
/ /		
/ /		Death
/ /		Burial

535 Name 7x-Great-Grandmother

DATE	SOURCE	INFORMATION
/ /		Birth
/ /		Baptism
/ /		
/ /		
/ /		
/ /		
/ /		
/ /		
/ /		
/ /		
/ /		Death
/ /		Burial

268 Name

6x-GREAT-GRANDFATHER

DATE	SOURCE	INFORMATION
/ /		Birth
/ /		Baptism
/ /		
/ /		
/ /		
/ /		
/ /		
/ /		
/ /		
/ /		
/ /		
/ /		
/ /		
/ /		
/ /		Death
/ /		Burial

...the child of...

536 Name

7x-GREAT-GRANDFATHER

DATE	SOURCE	INFORMATION
/ /		Birth
/ /		Baptism
/ /		
/ /		
/ /		
/ /		
/ /		
/ /		
/ /		
/ /		
/ /		Death
/ /		Burial

537 Name

7x-GREAT-GRANDMOTHER

DATE	SOURCE	INFORMATION
/ /		Birth
/ /		Baptism
/ /		
/ /		
/ /		
/ /		
/ /		
/ /		
/ /		
/ /		
/ /		Death
/ /		Burial

6x-Great-Grandmother

Name 269

DATE	SOURCE	INFORMATION
/ /		Birth
/ /		Baptism
/ /		
/ /		
/ /		
/ /		
/ /		
/ /		
/ /		
/ /		
/ /		
/ /		
/ /		
/ /		
/ /		Death
/ /		Burial

...the child of...

538 Name 7x-Great-Grandfather

DATE	SOURCE	INFORMATION
/ /		Birth
/ /		Baptism
/ /		
/ /		
/ /		
/ /		
/ /		
/ /		
/ /		
/ /		
/ /		Death
/ /		Burial

539 Name 7x-Great-Grandmother

DATE	SOURCE	INFORMATION
/ /		Birth
/ /		Baptism
/ /		
/ /		
/ /		
/ /		
/ /		
/ /		
/ /		
/ /		
/ /		Death
/ /		Burial

270 Name

6x-Great-Grandfather

DATE	SOURCE	INFORMATION
/ /		Birth
/ /		Baptism
/ /		
/ /		
/ /		
/ /		
/ /		
/ /		
/ /		
/ /		
/ /		
/ /		
/ /		
/ /		
/ /		Death
/ /		Burial

...the child of...

540 Name

7x-Great-Grandfather

DATE	SOURCE	INFORMATION
/ /		Birth
/ /		Baptism
/ /		
/ /		
/ /		
/ /		
/ /		
/ /		
/ /		
/ /		
/ /		Death
/ /		Burial

541 Name

7x-Great-Grandmother

DATE	SOURCE	INFORMATION
/ /		Birth
/ /		Baptism
/ /		
/ /		
/ /		
/ /		
/ /		
/ /		
/ /		
/ /		
/ /		Death
/ /		Burial

Name 271

DATE	SOURCE	INFORMATION
/ /		Birth
/ /		Baptism
/ /		
/ /		
/ /		
/ /		
/ /		
/ /		
/ /		
/ /		
/ /		
/ /		
/ /		
/ /		
/ /		Death
/ /		Burial

...the child of...

542 **Name** 7x-Great-Grandfather

DATE	SOURCE	INFORMATION
/ /		Birth
/ /		Baptism
/ /		
/ /		
/ /		
/ /		
/ /		
/ /		
/ /		
/ /		
/ /		Death
/ /		Burial

543 **Name** 7x-Great-Grandmother

DATE	SOURCE	INFORMATION
/ /		Birth
/ /		Baptism
/ /		
/ /		
/ /		
/ /		
/ /		
/ /		
/ /		
/ /		
/ /		Death
/ /		Burial

272 Name

6x-Great-Grandfather

DATE	SOURCE	INFORMATION
/ /		Birth
/ /		Baptism
/ /		
/ /		
/ /		
/ /		
/ /		
/ /		
/ /		
/ /		
/ /		
/ /		
/ /		
/ /		
/ /		Death
/ /		Burial

...the child of...

544 Name

7x-Great-Grandfather

DATE	SOURCE	INFORMATION
/ /		Birth
/ /		Baptism
/ /		
/ /		
/ /		
/ /		
/ /		
/ /		
/ /		
/ /		
/ /		Death
/ /		Burial

545 Name

7x-Great-Grandmother

DATE	SOURCE	INFORMATION
/ /		Birth
/ /		Baptism
/ /		
/ /		
/ /		
/ /		
/ /		
/ /		
/ /		
/ /		
/ /		Death
/ /		Burial

6x-Great-Grandmother

Name 273

DATE	SOURCE	INFORMATION
/ /		Birth
/ /		Baptism
/ /		
/ /		
/ /		
/ /		
/ /		
/ /		
/ /		
/ /		
/ /		
/ /		
/ /		
/ /		
/ /		Death
/ /		Burial

...the child of...

546 **Name** 7x-Great-Grandfather

DATE	SOURCE	INFORMATION
/ /		Birth
/ /		Baptism
/ /		
/ /		
/ /		
/ /		
/ /		
/ /		
/ /		
/ /		
/ /		Death
/ /		Burial

547 **Name** 7x-Great-Grandmother

DATE	SOURCE	INFORMATION
/ /		Birth
/ /		Baptism
/ /		
/ /		
/ /		
/ /		
/ /		
/ /		
/ /		
/ /		
/ /		Death
/ /		Burial

274 Name

6x-Great-Grandfather

DATE	SOURCE	INFORMATION
/ /		Birth
/ /		Baptism
/ /		
/ /		
/ /		
/ /		
/ /		
/ /		
/ /		
/ /		
/ /		
/ /		
/ /		
/ /		
/ /		Death
/ /		Burial

...the child of...

548 Name

7x-Great-Grandfather

DATE	SOURCE	INFORMATION
/ /		Birth
/ /		Baptism
/ /		
/ /		
/ /		
/ /		
/ /		
/ /		
/ /		
/ /		
/ /		Death
/ /		Burial

549 Name

7x-Great-Grandmother

DATE	SOURCE	INFORMATION
/ /		Birth
/ /		Baptism
/ /		
/ /		
/ /		
/ /		
/ /		
/ /		
/ /		
/ /		
/ /		Death
/ /		Burial

Name 275

DATE	SOURCE	INFORMATION
/ /		Birth
/ /		Baptism
/ /		
/ /		
/ /		
/ /		
/ /		
/ /		
/ /		
/ /		
/ /		
/ /		
/ /		
/ /		
/ /		Death
/ /		Burial

...the child of...

550 Name 7x-Great-Grandfather

DATE	SOURCE	INFORMATION
/ /		Birth
/ /		Baptism
/ /		
/ /		
/ /		
/ /		
/ /		
/ /		
/ /		
/ /		
/ /		Death
/ /		Burial

551 Name 7x-Great-Grandmother

DATE	SOURCE	INFORMATION
/ /		Birth
/ /		Baptism
/ /		
/ /		
/ /		
/ /		
/ /		
/ /		
/ /		
/ /		
/ /		Death
/ /		Burial

276 Name

6x-Great-Grandfather

DATE	SOURCE	INFORMATION
/ /		Birth
/ /		Baptism
/ /		
/ /		
/ /		
/ /		
/ /		
/ /		
/ /		
/ /		
/ /		
/ /		
/ /		
/ /		
/ /		Death
/ /		Burial

...the child of...

552 Name

7x-Great-Grandfather

DATE	SOURCE	INFORMATION
/ /		Birth
/ /		Baptism
/ /		
/ /		
/ /		
/ /		
/ /		
/ /		
/ /		
/ /		
/ /		Death
/ /		Burial

553 Name

7x-Great-Grandmother

DATE	SOURCE	INFORMATION
/ /		Birth
/ /		Baptism
/ /		
/ /		
/ /		
/ /		
/ /		
/ /		
/ /		
/ /		
/ /		Death
/ /		Burial

Name 277

DATE	SOURCE	INFORMATION
/ /		Birth
/ /		Baptism
/ /		
/ /		
/ /		
/ /		
/ /		
/ /		
/ /		
/ /		
/ /		
/ /		
/ /		
/ /		
/ /		Death
/ /		Burial

...the child of...

554 **Name** 7x-Great-Grandfather

DATE	SOURCE	INFORMATION
/ /		Birth
/ /		Baptism
/ /		
/ /		
/ /		
/ /		
/ /		
/ /		
/ /		
/ /		
/ /		Death
/ /		Burial

555 **Name** 7x-Great-Grandmother

DATE	SOURCE	INFORMATION
/ /		Birth
/ /		Baptism
/ /		
/ /		
/ /		
/ /		
/ /		
/ /		
/ /		
/ /		
/ /		Death
/ /		Burial

278 Name

6x-Great-Grandfather

DATE	SOURCE	INFORMATION
/ /		Birth
/ /		Baptism
/ /		
/ /		
/ /		
/ /		
/ /		
/ /		
/ /		
/ /		
/ /		
/ /		
/ /		
/ /		
/ /		Death
/ /		Burial

...the child of...

556 Name

7x-Great-Grandfather

DATE	SOURCE	INFORMATION
/ /		Birth
/ /		Baptism
/ /		
/ /		
/ /		
/ /		
/ /		
/ /		
/ /		
/ /		
/ /		Death
/ /		Burial

557 Name

7x-Great-Grandmother

DATE	SOURCE	INFORMATION
/ /		Birth
/ /		Baptism
/ /		
/ /		
/ /		
/ /		
/ /		
/ /		
/ /		
/ /		
/ /		Death
/ /		Burial

Name 279

DATE	SOURCE	INFORMATION
/ /		Birth
/ /		Baptism
/ /		
/ /		
/ /		
/ /		
/ /		
/ /		
/ /		
/ /		
/ /		
/ /		
/ /		
/ /		
/ /		Death
/ /		Burial

...the child of...

558 **Name** 7x-Great-Grandfather

DATE	SOURCE	INFORMATION
/ /		Birth
/ /		Baptism
/ /		
/ /		
/ /		
/ /		
/ /		
/ /		
/ /		
/ /		
/ /		Death
/ /		Burial

559 **Name** 7x-Great-Grandmother

DATE	SOURCE	INFORMATION
/ /		Birth
/ /		Baptism
/ /		
/ /		
/ /		
/ /		
/ /		
/ /		
/ /		
/ /		
/ /		Death
/ /		Burial

280 Name

6x-GREAT-GRANDFATHER

DATE	SOURCE	INFORMATION
/ /		Birth
/ /		Baptism
/ /		
/ /		
/ /		
/ /		
/ /		
/ /		
/ /		
/ /		
/ /		
/ /		
/ /		
/ /		
/ /		Death
/ /		Burial

...the child of...

560 Name

7x-GREAT-GRANDFATHER

DATE	SOURCE	INFORMATION
/ /		Birth
/ /		Baptism
/ /		
/ /		
/ /		
/ /		
/ /		
/ /		
/ /		
/ /		
/ /		Death
/ /		Burial

561 Name

7x-GREAT-GRANDMOTHER

DATE	SOURCE	INFORMATION
/ /		Birth
/ /		Baptism
/ /		
/ /		
/ /		
/ /		
/ /		
/ /		
/ /		
/ /		
/ /		Death
/ /		Burial

Name 281

DATE	SOURCE	INFORMATION
/ /		Birth
/ /		Baptism
/ /		
/ /		
/ /		
/ /		
/ /		
/ /		
/ /		
/ /		
/ /		
/ /		
/ /		
/ /		
/ /		Death
/ /		Burial

...the child of...

562 **Name** 7x-Great-Grandfather

DATE	SOURCE	INFORMATION
/ /		Birth
/ /		Baptism
/ /		
/ /		
/ /		
/ /		
/ /		
/ /		
/ /		
/ /		
/ /		Death
/ /		Burial

563 **Name** 7x-Great-Grandmother

DATE	SOURCE	INFORMATION
/ /		Birth
/ /		Baptism
/ /		
/ /		
/ /		
/ /		
/ /		
/ /		
/ /		
/ /		
/ /		Death
/ /		Burial

282 Name

6x-Great-Grandfather

DATE	SOURCE	INFORMATION
/ /		Birth
/ /		Baptism
/ /		
/ /		
/ /		
/ /		
/ /		
/ /		
/ /		
/ /		
/ /		
/ /		
/ /		
/ /		
/ /		Death
/ /		Burial

...the child of...

564 Name

7x-Great-Grandfather

DATE	SOURCE	INFORMATION
/ /		Birth
/ /		Baptism
/ /		
/ /		
/ /		
/ /		
/ /		
/ /		
/ /		
/ /		
/ /		Death
/ /		Burial

565 Name

7x-Great-Grandmother

DATE	SOURCE	INFORMATION
/ /		Birth
/ /		Baptism
/ /		
/ /		
/ /		
/ /		
/ /		
/ /		
/ /		
/ /		
/ /		Death
/ /		Burial

6x-Great-Grandmother

Name 283

DATE	SOURCE	INFORMATION
/ /		Birth
/ /		Baptism
/ /		
/ /		
/ /		
/ /		
/ /		
/ /		
/ /		
/ /		
/ /		
/ /		
/ /		
/ /		
/ /		Death
/ /		Burial

...the child of...

566 **Name** 7x-Great-Grandfather

DATE	SOURCE	INFORMATION
/ /		Birth
/ /		Baptism
/ /		
/ /		
/ /		
/ /		
/ /		
/ /		
/ /		
/ /		
/ /		Death
/ /		Burial

567 **Name** 7x-Great-Grandmother

DATE	SOURCE	INFORMATION
/ /		Birth
/ /		Baptism
/ /		
/ /		
/ /		
/ /		
/ /		
/ /		
/ /		
/ /		
/ /		Death
/ /		Burial

284 Name

6x-Great-Grandfather

DATE	SOURCE	INFORMATION
/ /		Birth
/ /		Baptism
/ /		
/ /		
/ /		
/ /		
/ /		
/ /		
/ /		
/ /		
/ /		
/ /		
/ /		
/ /		
/ /		Death
/ /		Burial

...the child of...

568 Name

7x-Great-Grandfather

DATE	SOURCE	INFORMATION
/ /		Birth
/ /		Baptism
/ /		
/ /		
/ /		
/ /		
/ /		
/ /		
/ /		
/ /		
/ /		Death
/ /		Burial

569 Name

7x-Great-Grandmother

DATE	SOURCE	INFORMATION
/ /		Birth
/ /		Baptism
/ /		
/ /		
/ /		
/ /		
/ /		
/ /		
/ /		
/ /		
/ /		Death
/ /		Burial

Name **285**

DATE	SOURCE	INFORMATION
/ /		Birth
/ /		Baptism
/ /		
/ /		
/ /		
/ /		
/ /		
/ /		
/ /		
/ /		
/ /		
/ /		
/ /		
/ /		
/ /		Death
/ /		Burial

...the child of...

570 Name 7x-Great-Grandfather

DATE	SOURCE	INFORMATION
/ /		Birth
/ /		Baptism
/ /		
/ /		
/ /		
/ /		
/ /		
/ /		
/ /		
/ /		
/ /		Death
/ /		Burial

571 Name 7x-Great-Grandmother

DATE	SOURCE	INFORMATION
/ /		Birth
/ /		Baptism
/ /		
/ /		
/ /		
/ /		
/ /		
/ /		
/ /		
/ /		
/ /		Death
/ /		Burial

286 Name

6x-Great-Grandfather

DATE	SOURCE	INFORMATION
/ /		Birth
/ /		Baptism
/ /		
/ /		
/ /		
/ /		
/ /		
/ /		
/ /		
/ /		
/ /		
/ /		
/ /		
/ /		
/ /		Death
/ /		Burial

...the child of...

572 Name

7x-Great-Grandfather

DATE	SOURCE	INFORMATION
/ /		Birth
/ /		Baptism
/ /		
/ /		
/ /		
/ /		
/ /		
/ /		
/ /		
/ /		
/ /		Death
/ /		Burial

573 Name

7x-Great-Grandmother

DATE	SOURCE	INFORMATION
/ /		Birth
/ /		Baptism
/ /		
/ /		
/ /		
/ /		
/ /		
/ /		
/ /		
/ /		
/ /		Death
/ /		Burial

Name 287

DATE	SOURCE	INFORMATION
/ /		Birth
/ /		Baptism
/ /		
/ /		
/ /		
/ /		
/ /		
/ /		
/ /		
/ /		
/ /		
/ /		
/ /		
/ /		
/ /		Death
/ /		Burial

...the child of...

574 **Name** 7x-Great-Grandfather

DATE	SOURCE	INFORMATION
/ /		Birth
/ /		Baptism
/ /		
/ /		
/ /		
/ /		
/ /		
/ /		
/ /		
/ /		
/ /		Death
/ /		Burial

575 **Name** 7x-Great-Grandmother

DATE	SOURCE	INFORMATION
/ /		Birth
/ /		Baptism
/ /		
/ /		
/ /		
/ /		
/ /		
/ /		
/ /		
/ /		
/ /		Death
/ /		Burial

288 Name

6x-Great-Grandfather

DATE	SOURCE	INFORMATION
/ /		Birth
/ /		Baptism
/ /		
/ /		
/ /		
/ /		
/ /		
/ /		
/ /		
/ /		
/ /		
/ /		
/ /		
/ /		
/ /		Death
/ /		Burial

...the child of...

576 Name

7x-Great-Grandfather

DATE	SOURCE	INFORMATION
/ /		Birth
/ /		Baptism
/ /		
/ /		
/ /		
/ /		
/ /		
/ /		
/ /		
/ /		
/ /		Death
/ /		Burial

577 Name

7x-Great-Grandmother

DATE	SOURCE	INFORMATION
/ /		Birth
/ /		Baptism
/ /		
/ /		
/ /		
/ /		
/ /		
/ /		
/ /		
/ /		
/ /		Death
/ /		Burial

6x-Great-Grandmother **Name 289**

DATE	SOURCE	INFORMATION
/ /		Birth
/ /		Baptism
/ /		
/ /		
/ /		
/ /		
/ /		
/ /		
/ /		
/ /		
/ /		
/ /		
/ /		
/ /		
/ /		Death
/ /		Burial

...the child of...

578 **Name** 7x-Great-Grandfather

DATE	SOURCE	INFORMATION
/ /		Birth
/ /		Baptism
/ /		
/ /		
/ /		
/ /		
/ /		
/ /		
/ /		
/ /		
/ /		Death
/ /		Burial

579 **Name** 7x-Great-Grandmother

DATE	SOURCE	INFORMATION
/ /		Birth
/ /		Baptism
/ /		
/ /		
/ /		
/ /		
/ /		
/ /		
/ /		
/ /		
/ /		Death
/ /		Burial

290 Name

6x-Great-Grandfather

DATE	SOURCE	INFORMATION
/ /		Birth
/ /		Baptism
/ /		
/ /		
/ /		
/ /		
/ /		
/ /		
/ /		
/ /		
/ /		
/ /		
/ /		
/ /		
/ /		Death
/ /		Burial

…the child of…

580 Name

7x-Great-Grandfather

DATE	SOURCE	INFORMATION
/ /		Birth
/ /		Baptism
/ /		
/ /		
/ /		
/ /		
/ /		
/ /		
/ /		
/ /		
/ /		Death
/ /		Burial

581 Name

7x-Great-Grandmother

DATE	SOURCE	INFORMATION
/ /		Birth
/ /		Baptism
/ /		
/ /		
/ /		
/ /		
/ /		
/ /		
/ /		
/ /		
/ /		Death
/ /		Burial

Name 291

DATE	SOURCE	INFORMATION
/ /		Birth
/ /		Baptism
/ /		
/ /		
/ /		
/ /		
/ /		
/ /		
/ /		
/ /		
/ /		
/ /		
/ /		
/ /		
/ /		Death
/ /		Burial

...the child of...

582 **Name** 7x-Great-Grandfather

DATE	SOURCE	INFORMATION
/ /		Birth
/ /		Baptism
/ /		
/ /		
/ /		
/ /		
/ /		
/ /		
/ /		
/ /		
/ /		Death
/ /		Burial

583 **Name** 7x-Great-Grandmother

DATE	SOURCE	INFORMATION
/ /		Birth
/ /		Baptism
/ /		
/ /		
/ /		
/ /		
/ /		
/ /		
/ /		
/ /		
/ /		Death
/ /		Burial

292 Name

6x-Great-Grandfather

DATE	SOURCE	INFORMATION
/ /		Birth
/ /		Baptism
/ /		
/ /		
/ /		
/ /		
/ /		
/ /		
/ /		
/ /		
/ /		
/ /		
/ /		
/ /		
/ /		Death
/ /		Burial

...the child of...

584 Name

7x-Great-Grandfather

DATE	SOURCE	INFORMATION
/ /		Birth
/ /		Baptism
/ /		
/ /		
/ /		
/ /		
/ /		
/ /		
/ /		
/ /		
/ /		Death
/ /		Burial

585 Name

7x-Great-Grandmother

DATE	SOURCE	INFORMATION
/ /		Birth
/ /		Baptism
/ /		
/ /		
/ /		
/ /		
/ /		
/ /		
/ /		
/ /		
/ /		Death
/ /		Burial

Name 293

DATE	SOURCE	INFORMATION
/ /		Birth
/ /		Baptism
/ /		
/ /		
/ /		
/ /		
/ /		
/ /		
/ /		
/ /		
/ /		
/ /		
/ /		
/ /		
/ /		Death
/ /		Burial

...the child of...

586 **Name** 7x-Great-Grandfather

DATE	SOURCE	INFORMATION
/ /		Birth
/ /		Baptism
/ /		
/ /		
/ /		
/ /		
/ /		
/ /		
/ /		
/ /		
/ /		Death
/ /		Burial

587 **Name** 7x-Great-Grandmother

DATE	SOURCE	INFORMATION
/ /		Birth
/ /		Baptism
/ /		
/ /		
/ /		
/ /		
/ /		
/ /		
/ /		
/ /		
/ /		Death
/ /		Burial

294 Name

6x-Great-Grandfather

DATE	SOURCE	INFORMATION
/ /		Birth
/ /		Baptism
/ /		
/ /		
/ /		
/ /		
/ /		
/ /		
/ /		
/ /		
/ /		
/ /		
/ /		
/ /		
/ /		Death
/ /		Burial

...the child of...

588 Name

7x-Great-Grandfather

DATE	SOURCE	INFORMATION
/ /		Birth
/ /		Baptism
/ /		
/ /		
/ /		
/ /		
/ /		
/ /		
/ /		
/ /		
/ /		Death
/ /		Burial

589 Name

7x-Great-Grandmother

DATE	SOURCE	INFORMATION
/ /		Birth
/ /		Baptism
/ /		
/ /		
/ /		
/ /		
/ /		
/ /		
/ /		
/ /		
/ /		Death
/ /		Burial

Name 295

DATE	SOURCE	INFORMATION
/ /		Birth
/ /		Baptism
/ /		
/ /		
/ /		
/ /		
/ /		
/ /		
/ /		
/ /		
/ /		
/ /		
/ /		
/ /		
/ /		Death
/ /		Burial

...the child of...

590 **Name** 7x-Great-Grandfather

DATE	SOURCE	INFORMATION
/ /		Birth
/ /		Baptism
/ /		
/ /		
/ /		
/ /		
/ /		
/ /		
/ /		
/ /		
/ /		Death
/ /		Burial

591 **Name** 7x-Great-Grandmother

DATE	SOURCE	INFORMATION
/ /		Birth
/ /		Baptism
/ /		
/ /		
/ /		
/ /		
/ /		
/ /		
/ /		
/ /		
/ /		Death
/ /		Burial

296 Name

6x-Great-Grandfather

DATE	SOURCE	INFORMATION
/ /		Birth
/ /		Baptism
/ /		
/ /		
/ /		
/ /		
/ /		
/ /		
/ /		
/ /		
/ /		
/ /		
/ /		
/ /		
/ /		Death
/ /		Burial

...the child of...

592 Name

7x-Great-Grandfather

DATE	SOURCE	INFORMATION
/ /		Birth
/ /		Baptism
/ /		
/ /		
/ /		
/ /		
/ /		
/ /		
/ /		
/ /		
/ /		Death
/ /		Burial

593 Name

7x-Great-Grandmother

DATE	SOURCE	INFORMATION
/ /		Birth
/ /		Baptism
/ /		
/ /		
/ /		
/ /		
/ /		
/ /		
/ /		
/ /		
/ /		Death
/ /		Burial

Name 297

DATE	SOURCE	INFORMATION
/ /		Birth
/ /		Baptism
/ /		
/ /		
/ /		
/ /		
/ /		
/ /		
/ /		
/ /		
/ /		
/ /		
/ /		
/ /		
/ /		Death
/ /		Burial

...the child of...

594 **Name** 7x-Great-Grandfather

DATE	SOURCE	INFORMATION
/ /		Birth
/ /		Baptism
/ /		
/ /		
/ /		
/ /		
/ /		
/ /		
/ /		
/ /		
/ /		Death
/ /		Burial

595 **Name** 7x-Great-Grandmother

DATE	SOURCE	INFORMATION
/ /		Birth
/ /		Baptism
/ /		
/ /		
/ /		
/ /		
/ /		
/ /		
/ /		
/ /		
/ /		Death
/ /		Burial

298 Name

6x-Great-Grandfather

DATE	SOURCE	INFORMATION
/ /		Birth
/ /		Baptism
/ /		
/ /		
/ /		
/ /		
/ /		
/ /		
/ /		
/ /		
/ /		
/ /		
/ /		
/ /		
/ /		Death
/ /		Burial

...the child of...

596 Name

7x-Great-Grandfather

DATE	SOURCE	INFORMATION
/ /		Birth
/ /		Baptism
/ /		
/ /		
/ /		
/ /		
/ /		
/ /		
/ /		
/ /		
/ /		Death
/ /		Burial

597 Name

7x-Great-Grandmother

DATE	SOURCE	INFORMATION
/ /		Birth
/ /		Baptism
/ /		
/ /		
/ /		
/ /		
/ /		
/ /		
/ /		
/ /		
/ /		Death
/ /		Burial

6x-Great-Grandmother

Name 299

DATE	SOURCE	INFORMATION
/ /		Birth
/ /		Baptism
/ /		
/ /		
/ /		
/ /		
/ /		
/ /		
/ /		
/ /		
/ /		
/ /		
/ /		
/ /		
/ /		Death
/ /		Burial

...the child of...

598 **Name** 7x-Great-Grandfather

DATE	SOURCE	INFORMATION
/ /		Birth
/ /		Baptism
/ /		
/ /		
/ /		
/ /		
/ /		
/ /		
/ /		
/ /		
/ /		Death
/ /		Burial

599 **Name** 7x-Great-Grandmother

DATE	SOURCE	INFORMATION
/ /		Birth
/ /		Baptism
/ /		
/ /		
/ /		
/ /		
/ /		
/ /		
/ /		
/ /		
/ /		Death
/ /		Burial

300 Name

6x-Great-Grandfather

DATE	SOURCE	INFORMATION
/ /		Birth
/ /		Baptism
/ /		
/ /		
/ /		
/ /		
/ /		
/ /		
/ /		
/ /		
/ /		
/ /		
/ /		
/ /		
/ /		Death
/ /		Burial

...the child of...

600 Name

7x-Great-Grandfather

DATE	SOURCE	INFORMATION
/ /		Birth
/ /		Baptism
/ /		
/ /		
/ /		
/ /		
/ /		
/ /		
/ /		
/ /		
/ /		Death
/ /		Burial

601 Name

7x-Great-Grandmother

DATE	SOURCE	INFORMATION
/ /		Birth
/ /		Baptism
/ /		
/ /		
/ /		
/ /		
/ /		
/ /		
/ /		
/ /		
/ /		Death
/ /		Burial

Name 301

DATE	SOURCE	INFORMATION
/ /		Birth
/ /		Baptism
/ /		
/ /		
/ /		
/ /		
/ /		
/ /		
/ /		
/ /		
/ /		
/ /		
/ /		
/ /		
/ /		Death
/ /		Burial

...the child of...

602 **Name** 7x-Great-Grandfather

DATE	SOURCE	INFORMATION
/ /		Birth
/ /		Baptism
/ /		
/ /		
/ /		
/ /		
/ /		
/ /		
/ /		
/ /		
/ /		Death
/ /		Burial

603 **Name** 7x-Great-Grandmother

DATE	SOURCE	INFORMATION
/ /		Birth
/ /		Baptism
/ /		
/ /		
/ /		
/ /		
/ /		
/ /		
/ /		
/ /		
/ /		Death
/ /		Burial

302 Name

6x-Great-Grandfather

DATE	SOURCE	INFORMATION
/ /		Birth
/ /		Baptism
/ /		
/ /		
/ /		
/ /		
/ /		
/ /		
/ /		
/ /		
/ /		
/ /		
/ /		
/ /		
/ /		Death
/ /		Burial

...the child of...

604 Name

7x-Great-Grandfather

DATE	SOURCE	INFORMATION
/ /		Birth
/ /		Baptism
/ /		
/ /		
/ /		
/ /		
/ /		
/ /		
/ /		
/ /		
/ /		Death
/ /		Burial

605 Name

7x-Great-Grandmother

DATE	SOURCE	INFORMATION
/ /		Birth
/ /		Baptism
/ /		
/ /		
/ /		
/ /		
/ /		
/ /		
/ /		
/ /		
/ /		Death
/ /		Burial

Name 303

DATE	SOURCE	INFORMATION
/ /		Birth
/ /		Baptism
/ /		
/ /		
/ /		
/ /		
/ /		
/ /		
/ /		
/ /		
/ /		
/ /		
/ /		
/ /		
/ /		Death
/ /		Burial

...the child of...

606 **Name** 7x-Great-Grandfather

DATE	SOURCE	INFORMATION
/ /		Birth
/ /		Baptism
/ /		
/ /		
/ /		
/ /		
/ /		
/ /		
/ /		
/ /		
/ /		Death
/ /		Burial

607 **Name** 7x-Great-Grandmother

DATE	SOURCE	INFORMATION
/ /		Birth
/ /		Baptism
/ /		
/ /		
/ /		
/ /		
/ /		
/ /		
/ /		
/ /		
/ /		Death
/ /		Burial

304 Name

6x-Great-Grandfather

DATE	SOURCE	INFORMATION
/ /		Birth
/ /		Baptism
/ /		
/ /		
/ /		
/ /		
/ /		
/ /		
/ /		
/ /		
/ /		
/ /		
/ /		
/ /		
/ /		Death
/ /		Burial

...the child of...

608 Name

7x-Great-Grandfather

DATE	SOURCE	INFORMATION
/ /		Birth
/ /		Baptism
/ /		
/ /		
/ /		
/ /		
/ /		
/ /		
/ /		
/ /		
/ /		Death
/ /		Burial

609 Name

7x-Great-Grandmother

DATE	SOURCE	INFORMATION
/ /		Birth
/ /		Baptism
/ /		
/ /		
/ /		
/ /		
/ /		
/ /		
/ /		
/ /		
/ /		Death
/ /		Burial

Name 305

DATE	SOURCE	INFORMATION
/ /		Birth
/ /		Baptism
/ /		
/ /		
/ /		
/ /		
/ /		
/ /		
/ /		
/ /		
/ /		
/ /		
/ /		
/ /		
/ /		Death
/ /		Burial

...the child of...

610 **Name** 7x-Great-Grandfather

DATE	SOURCE	INFORMATION
/ /		Birth
/ /		Baptism
/ /		
/ /		
/ /		
/ /		
/ /		
/ /		
/ /		
/ /		
/ /		Death
/ /		Burial

611 **Name** 7x-Great-Grandmother

DATE	SOURCE	INFORMATION
/ /		Birth
/ /		Baptism
/ /		
/ /		
/ /		
/ /		
/ /		
/ /		
/ /		
/ /		
/ /		Death
/ /		Burial

306 Name

6x-Great-Grandfather

DATE	SOURCE	INFORMATION
/ /		Birth
/ /		Baptism
/ /		
/ /		
/ /		
/ /		
/ /		
/ /		
/ /		
/ /		
/ /		
/ /		
/ /		
/ /		
/ /		Death
/ /		Burial

...the child of...

612 Name

7x-Great-Grandfather

DATE	SOURCE	INFORMATION
/ /		Birth
/ /		Baptism
/ /		
/ /		
/ /		
/ /		
/ /		
/ /		
/ /		
/ /		
/ /		Death
/ /		Burial

613 Name

7x-Great-Grandmother

DATE	SOURCE	INFORMATION
/ /		Birth
/ /		Baptism
/ /		
/ /		
/ /		
/ /		
/ /		
/ /		
/ /		
/ /		
/ /		Death
/ /		Burial

Name 307

DATE	SOURCE	INFORMATION
/ /		Birth
/ /		Baptism
/ /		
/ /		
/ /		
/ /		
/ /		
/ /		
/ /		
/ /		
/ /		
/ /		
/ /		
/ /		
/ /		Death
/ /		Burial

...the child of...

614 **Name** 7x-Great-Grandfather

DATE	SOURCE	INFORMATION
/ /		Birth
/ /		Baptism
/ /		
/ /		
/ /		
/ /		
/ /		
/ /		
/ /		
/ /		
/ /		Death
/ /		Burial

615 **Name** 7x-Great-Grandmother

DATE	SOURCE	INFORMATION
/ /		Birth
/ /		Baptism
/ /		
/ /		
/ /		
/ /		
/ /		
/ /		
/ /		
/ /		
/ /		Death
/ /		Burial

308 Name

6x-Great-Grandfather

DATE	SOURCE	INFORMATION
/ /		Birth
/ /		Baptism
/ /		
/ /		
/ /		
/ /		
/ /		
/ /		
/ /		
/ /		
/ /		
/ /		
/ /		
/ /		
/ /		Death
/ /		Burial

...the child of...

616 Name

7x-Great-Grandfather

DATE	SOURCE	INFORMATION
/ /		Birth
/ /		Baptism
/ /		
/ /		
/ /		
/ /		
/ /		
/ /		
/ /		
/ /		
/ /		Death
/ /		Burial

617 Name

7x-Great-Grandmother

DATE	SOURCE	INFORMATION
/ /		Birth
/ /		Baptism
/ /		
/ /		
/ /		
/ /		
/ /		
/ /		
/ /		
/ /		
/ /		Death
/ /		Burial

Name 309

DATE	SOURCE	INFORMATION
/ /		Birth
/ /		Baptism
/ /		
/ /		
/ /		
/ /		
/ /		
/ /		
/ /		
/ /		
/ /		
/ /		
/ /		
/ /		
/ /		Death
/ /		Burial

...the child of...

618 **Name** 7x-Great-Grandfather

DATE	SOURCE	INFORMATION
/ /		Birth
/ /		Baptism
/ /		
/ /		
/ /		
/ /		
/ /		
/ /		
/ /		
/ /		
/ /		Death
/ /		Burial

619 **Name** 7x-Great-Grandmother

DATE	SOURCE	INFORMATION
/ /		Birth
/ /		Baptism
/ /		
/ /		
/ /		
/ /		
/ /		
/ /		
/ /		
/ /		
/ /		Death
/ /		Burial

310 Name

6x-Great-Grandfather

DATE	SOURCE	INFORMATION
/ /		Birth
/ /		Baptism
/ /		
/ /		
/ /		
/ /		
/ /		
/ /		
/ /		
/ /		
/ /		
/ /		
/ /		
/ /		
/ /		Death
/ /		Burial

...the child of...

620 Name

7x-Great-Grandfather

DATE	SOURCE	INFORMATION
/ /		Birth
/ /		Baptism
/ /		
/ /		
/ /		
/ /		
/ /		
/ /		
/ /		
/ /		
/ /		Death
/ /		Burial

621 Name

7x-Great-Grandmother

DATE	SOURCE	INFORMATION
/ /		Birth
/ /		Baptism
/ /		
/ /		
/ /		
/ /		
/ /		
/ /		
/ /		
/ /		
/ /		Death
/ /		Burial

6x-Great-Grandmother

Name 311

DATE	SOURCE	INFORMATION
/ /		Birth
/ /		Baptism
/ /		
/ /		
/ /		
/ /		
/ /		
/ /		
/ /		
/ /		
/ /		
/ /		
/ /		
/ /		
/ /		Death
/ /		Burial

...the child of...

622 **Name** 7x-Great-Grandfather

DATE	SOURCE	INFORMATION
/ /		Birth
/ /		Baptism
/ /		
/ /		
/ /		
/ /		
/ /		
/ /		
/ /		
/ /		
/ /		Death
/ /		Burial

623 **Name** 7x-Great-Grandmother

DATE	SOURCE	INFORMATION
/ /		Birth
/ /		Baptism
/ /		
/ /		
/ /		
/ /		
/ /		
/ /		
/ /		
/ /		
/ /		Death
/ /		Burial

312 Name

6x-Great-Grandfather

DATE	SOURCE	INFORMATION
/ /		Birth
/ /		Baptism
/ /		
/ /		
/ /		
/ /		
/ /		
/ /		
/ /		
/ /		
/ /		
/ /		
/ /		
/ /		
/ /		Death
/ /		Burial

...the child of...

624 Name

7x-Great-Grandfather

DATE	SOURCE	INFORMATION
/ /		Birth
/ /		Baptism
/ /		
/ /		
/ /		
/ /		
/ /		
/ /		
/ /		
/ /		
/ /		Death
/ /		Burial

625 Name

7x-Great-Grandmother

DATE	SOURCE	INFORMATION
/ /		Birth
/ /		Baptism
/ /		
/ /		
/ /		
/ /		
/ /		
/ /		
/ /		
/ /		
/ /		Death
/ /		Burial

6x-Great-Grandmother **Name 313**

DATE	SOURCE	INFORMATION
/ /		Birth
/ /		Baptism
/ /		
/ /		
/ /		
/ /		
/ /		
/ /		
/ /		
/ /		
/ /		
/ /		
/ /		
/ /		
/ /		Death
/ /		Burial

...the child of...

626 **Name** 7x-Great-Grandfather

DATE	SOURCE	INFORMATION
/ /		Birth
/ /		Baptism
/ /		
/ /		
/ /		
/ /		
/ /		
/ /		
/ /		
/ /		
/ /		Death
/ /		Burial

627 **Name** 7x-Great-Grandmother

DATE	SOURCE	INFORMATION
/ /		Birth
/ /		Baptism
/ /		
/ /		
/ /		
/ /		
/ /		
/ /		
/ /		
/ /		
/ /		Death
/ /		Burial

314 Name

6x-Great-Grandfather

DATE	SOURCE	INFORMATION
/ /		Birth
/ /		Baptism
/ /		
/ /		
/ /		
/ /		
/ /		
/ /		
/ /		
/ /		
/ /		
/ /		
/ /		
/ /		
/ /		Death
/ /		Burial

...the child of...

628 Name

7x-Great-Grandfather

DATE	SOURCE	INFORMATION
/ /		Birth
/ /		Baptism
/ /		
/ /		
/ /		
/ /		
/ /		
/ /		
/ /		
/ /		
/ /		Death
/ /		Burial

629 Name

7x-Great-Grandmother

DATE	SOURCE	INFORMATION
/ /		Birth
/ /		Baptism
/ /		
/ /		
/ /		
/ /		
/ /		
/ /		
/ /		
/ /		
/ /		Death
/ /		Burial

6x-Great-Grandmother

Name 315

DATE	SOURCE	INFORMATION
/ /		Birth
/ /		Baptism
/ /		
/ /		
/ /		
/ /		
/ /		
/ /		
/ /		
/ /		
/ /		
/ /		
/ /		
/ /		
/ /		Death
/ /		Burial

...the child of...

630 Name 7x-Great-Grandfather

DATE	SOURCE	INFORMATION
/ /		Birth
/ /		Baptism
/ /		
/ /		
/ /		
/ /		
/ /		
/ /		
/ /		
/ /		
/ /		Death
/ /		Burial

631 Name 7x-Great-Grandmother

DATE	SOURCE	INFORMATION
/ /		Birth
/ /		Baptism
/ /		
/ /		
/ /		
/ /		
/ /		
/ /		
/ /		
/ /		
/ /		Death
/ /		Burial

316 Name

6x-Great-Grandfather

DATE	SOURCE	INFORMATION
/ /		Birth
/ /		Baptism
/ /		
/ /		
/ /		
/ /		
/ /		
/ /		
/ /		
/ /		
/ /		
/ /		
/ /		
/ /		
/ /		Death
/ /		Burial

...the child of...

632 Name

7x-Great-Grandfather

DATE	SOURCE	INFORMATION
/ /		Birth
/ /		Baptism
/ /		
/ /		
/ /		
/ /		
/ /		
/ /		
/ /		
/ /		
/ /		Death
/ /		Burial

633 Name

7x-Great-Grandmother

DATE	SOURCE	INFORMATION
/ /		Birth
/ /		Baptism
/ /		
/ /		
/ /		
/ /		
/ /		
/ /		
/ /		
/ /		
/ /		Death
/ /		Burial

6x-Great-Grandmother

Name 317

DATE	SOURCE	INFORMATION
/ /		Birth
/ /		Baptism
/ /		
/ /		
/ /		
/ /		
/ /		
/ /		
/ /		
/ /		
/ /		
/ /		
/ /		
/ /		
/ /		Death
/ /		Burial

...the child of...

634 **Name** 7x-Great-Grandfather

DATE	SOURCE	INFORMATION
/ /		Birth
/ /		Baptism
/ /		
/ /		
/ /		
/ /		
/ /		
/ /		
/ /		
/ /		
/ /		Death
/ /		Burial

635 **Name** 7x-Great-Grandmother

DATE	SOURCE	INFORMATION
/ /		Birth
/ /		Baptism
/ /		
/ /		
/ /		
/ /		
/ /		
/ /		
/ /		
/ /		
/ /		Death
/ /		Burial

318 Name

6x-Great-Grandfather

DATE	SOURCE	INFORMATION
/ /		Birth
/ /		Baptism
/ /		
/ /		
/ /		
/ /		
/ /		
/ /		
/ /		
/ /		
/ /		
/ /		
/ /		
/ /		
/ /		Death
/ /		Burial

...the child of...

636 Name

7x-Great-Grandfather

DATE	SOURCE	INFORMATION
/ /		Birth
/ /		Baptism
/ /		
/ /		
/ /		
/ /		
/ /		
/ /		
/ /		
/ /		
/ /		Death
/ /		Burial

637 Name

7x-Great-Grandmother

DATE	SOURCE	INFORMATION
/ /		Birth
/ /		Baptism
/ /		
/ /		
/ /		
/ /		
/ /		
/ /		
/ /		
/ /		
/ /		Death
/ /		Burial

6x-Great-Grandmother

Name 319

DATE	SOURCE	INFORMATION
/ /		Birth
/ /		Baptism
/ /		
/ /		
/ /		
/ /		
/ /		
/ /		
/ /		
/ /		
/ /		
/ /		
/ /		
/ /		
/ /		Death
/ /		Burial

...the child of...

638 **Name** 7x-Great-Grandfather

DATE	SOURCE	INFORMATION
/ /		Birth
/ /		Baptism
/ /		
/ /		
/ /		
/ /		
/ /		
/ /		
/ /		
/ /		
/ /		Death
/ /		Burial

639 **Name** 7x-Great-Grandmother

DATE	SOURCE	INFORMATION
/ /		Birth
/ /		Baptism
/ /		
/ /		
/ /		
/ /		
/ /		
/ /		
/ /		
/ /		
/ /		Death
/ /		Burial

320 Name

6X-GREAT-GRANDFATHER

DATE	SOURCE	INFORMATION
/ /		Birth
/ /		Baptism
/ /		
/ /		
/ /		
/ /		
/ /		
/ /		
/ /		
/ /		
/ /		
/ /		
/ /		
/ /		
/ /		Death
/ /		Burial

...the child of...

640 Name

7X-GREAT-GRANDFATHER

DATE	SOURCE	INFORMATION
/ /		Birth
/ /		Baptism
/ /		
/ /		
/ /		
/ /		
/ /		
/ /		
/ /		
/ /		
/ /		Death
/ /		Burial

641 Name

7X-GREAT-GRANDMOTHER

DATE	SOURCE	INFORMATION
/ /		Birth
/ /		Baptism
/ /		
/ /		
/ /		
/ /		
/ /		
/ /		
/ /		
/ /		
/ /		Death
/ /		Burial

Name 321

DATE	SOURCE	INFORMATION
/ /		Birth
/ /		Baptism
/ /		
/ /		
/ /		
/ /		
/ /		
/ /		
/ /		
/ /		
/ /		
/ /		
/ /		
/ /		
/ /		Death
/ /		Burial

...the child of...

642 **Name** 7x-Great-Grandfather

DATE	SOURCE	INFORMATION
/ /		Birth
/ /		Baptism
/ /		
/ /		
/ /		
/ /		
/ /		
/ /		
/ /		
/ /		
/ /		Death
/ /		Burial

643 **Name** 7x-Great-Grandmother

DATE	SOURCE	INFORMATION
/ /		Birth
/ /		Baptism
/ /		
/ /		
/ /		
/ /		
/ /		
/ /		
/ /		
/ /		
/ /		Death
/ /		Burial

322 Name

6x-Great-Grandfather

DATE	SOURCE	INFORMATION
/ /		Birth
/ /		Baptism
/ /		
/ /		
/ /		
/ /		
/ /		
/ /		
/ /		
/ /		
/ /		
/ /		
/ /		
/ /		
/ /		Death
/ /		Burial

...the child of...

644 Name

7x-Great-Grandfather

DATE	SOURCE	INFORMATION
/ /		Birth
/ /		Baptism
/ /		
/ /		
/ /		
/ /		
/ /		
/ /		
/ /		
/ /		
/ /		Death
/ /		Burial

645 Name

7x-Great-Grandmother

DATE	SOURCE	INFORMATION
/ /		Birth
/ /		Baptism
/ /		
/ /		
/ /		
/ /		
/ /		
/ /		
/ /		
/ /		
/ /		Death
/ /		Burial

6x-Great-Grandmother

Name 323

DATE	SOURCE	INFORMATION
/ /		Birth
/ /		Baptism
/ /		
/ /		
/ /		
/ /		
/ /		
/ /		
/ /		
/ /		
/ /		
/ /		
/ /		
/ /		
/ /		Death
/ /		Burial

...the child of...

646 **Name** 7x-Great-Grandfather

DATE	SOURCE	INFORMATION
/ /		Birth
/ /		Baptism
/ /		
/ /		
/ /		
/ /		
/ /		
/ /		
/ /		
/ /		
/ /		Death
/ /		Burial

647 **Name** 7x-Great-Grandmother

DATE	SOURCE	INFORMATION
/ /		Birth
/ /		Baptism
/ /		
/ /		
/ /		
/ /		
/ /		
/ /		
/ /		
/ /		
/ /		Death
/ /		Burial

324 Name

6x-Great-Grandfather

DATE	SOURCE	INFORMATION
/ /		Birth
/ /		Baptism
/ /		
/ /		
/ /		
/ /		
/ /		
/ /		
/ /		
/ /		
/ /		
/ /		
/ /		
/ /		
/ /		Death
/ /		Burial

...the child of...

648 Name

7x-Great-Grandfather

DATE	SOURCE	INFORMATION
/ /		Birth
/ /		Baptism
/ /		
/ /		
/ /		
/ /		
/ /		
/ /		
/ /		
/ /		
/ /		Death
/ /		Burial

649 Name

7x-Great-Grandmother

DATE	SOURCE	INFORMATION
/ /		Birth
/ /		Baptism
/ /		
/ /		
/ /		
/ /		
/ /		
/ /		
/ /		
/ /		
/ /		Death
/ /		Burial

Name 325

DATE	SOURCE	INFORMATION
/ /		Birth
/ /		Baptism
/ /		
/ /		
/ /		
/ /		
/ /		
/ /		
/ /		
/ /		
/ /		
/ /		
/ /		
/ /		
/ /		Death
/ /		Burial

...the child of...

650 Name 7x-Great-Grandfather

DATE	SOURCE	INFORMATION
/ /		Birth
/ /		Baptism
/ /		
/ /		
/ /		
/ /		
/ /		
/ /		
/ /		
/ /		
/ /		Death
/ /		Burial

651 Name 7x-Great-Grandmother

DATE	SOURCE	INFORMATION
/ /		Birth
/ /		Baptism
/ /		
/ /		
/ /		
/ /		
/ /		
/ /		
/ /		
/ /		
/ /		Death
/ /		Burial

326 Name

6x-Great-Grandfather

DATE	SOURCE	INFORMATION
/ /		Birth
/ /		Baptism
/ /		
/ /		
/ /		
/ /		
/ /		
/ /		
/ /		
/ /		
/ /		
/ /		
/ /		
/ /		
/ /		Death
/ /		Burial

...the child of...

652 Name

7x-Great-Grandfather

DATE	SOURCE	INFORMATION
/ /		Birth
/ /		Baptism
/ /		
/ /		
/ /		
/ /		
/ /		
/ /		
/ /		
/ /		
/ /		Death
/ /		Burial

653 Name

7x-Great-Grandmother

DATE	SOURCE	INFORMATION
/ /		Birth
/ /		Baptism
/ /		
/ /		
/ /		
/ /		
/ /		
/ /		
/ /		
/ /		
/ /		Death
/ /		Burial

Name 327

DATE	SOURCE	INFORMATION
/ /		Birth
/ /		Baptism
/ /		
/ /		
/ /		
/ /		
/ /		
/ /		
/ /		
/ /		
/ /		
/ /		
/ /		
/ /		
/ /		Death
/ /		Burial

...the child of...

654 **Name** 7x-Great-Grandfather

DATE	SOURCE	INFORMATION
/ /		Birth
/ /		Baptism
/ /		
/ /		
/ /		
/ /		
/ /		
/ /		
/ /		
/ /		
/ /		Death
/ /		Burial

655 **Name** 7x-Great-Grandmother

DATE	SOURCE	INFORMATION
/ /		Birth
/ /		Baptism
/ /		
/ /		
/ /		
/ /		
/ /		
/ /		
/ /		
/ /		
/ /		Death
/ /		Burial

328 Name

6x-Great-Grandfather

DATE	SOURCE	INFORMATION
/ /		Birth
/ /		Baptism
/ /		
/ /		
/ /		
/ /		
/ /		
/ /		
/ /		
/ /		
/ /		
/ /		
/ /		
/ /		
/ /		Death
/ /		Burial

...the child of...

656 Name

7x-Great-Grandfather

DATE	SOURCE	INFORMATION
/ /		Birth
/ /		Baptism
/ /		
/ /		
/ /		
/ /		
/ /		
/ /		
/ /		
/ /		
/ /		Death
/ /		Burial

657 Name

7x-Great-Grandmother

DATE	SOURCE	INFORMATION
/ /		Birth
/ /		Baptism
/ /		
/ /		
/ /		
/ /		
/ /		
/ /		
/ /		
/ /		
/ /		Death
/ /		Burial

Name 329

DATE	SOURCE	INFORMATION
/ /		Birth
/ /		Baptism
/ /		
/ /		
/ /		
/ /		
/ /		
/ /		
/ /		
/ /		
/ /		
/ /		
/ /		
/ /		
/ /		Death
/ /		Burial

...the child of...

658 **Name** 7x-Great-Grandfather

DATE	SOURCE	INFORMATION
/ /		Birth
/ /		Baptism
/ /		
/ /		
/ /		
/ /		
/ /		
/ /		
/ /		
/ /		
/ /		Death
/ /		Burial

659 **Name** 7x-Great-Grandmother

DATE	SOURCE	INFORMATION
/ /		Birth
/ /		Baptism
/ /		
/ /		
/ /		
/ /		
/ /		
/ /		
/ /		
/ /		
/ /		Death
/ /		Burial

330 Name

6x-Great-Grandfather

DATE	SOURCE	INFORMATION
/ /		Birth
/ /		Baptism
/ /		
/ /		
/ /		
/ /		
/ /		
/ /		
/ /		
/ /		
/ /		
/ /		
/ /		
/ /		
/ /		Death
/ /		Burial

…the child of…

660 Name

7x-Great-Grandfather

DATE	SOURCE	INFORMATION
/ /		Birth
/ /		Baptism
/ /		
/ /		
/ /		
/ /		
/ /		
/ /		
/ /		
/ /		
/ /		Death
/ /		Burial

661 Name

7x-Great-Grandmother

DATE	SOURCE	INFORMATION
/ /		Birth
/ /		Baptism
/ /		
/ /		
/ /		
/ /		
/ /		
/ /		
/ /		
/ /		
/ /		Death
/ /		Burial

Name 331

DATE	SOURCE	INFORMATION
/ /		Birth
/ /		Baptism
/ /		
/ /		
/ /		
/ /		
/ /		
/ /		
/ /		
/ /		
/ /		
/ /		
/ /		
/ /		
/ /		Death
/ /		Burial

...the child of...

662 **Name** 7x-Great-Grandfather

DATE	SOURCE	INFORMATION
/ /		Birth
/ /		Baptism
/ /		
/ /		
/ /		
/ /		
/ /		
/ /		
/ /		
/ /		
/ /		Death
/ /		Burial

663 **Name** 7x-Great-Grandmother

DATE	SOURCE	INFORMATION
/ /		Birth
/ /		Baptism
/ /		
/ /		
/ /		
/ /		
/ /		
/ /		
/ /		
/ /		
/ /		Death
/ /		Burial

332 Name

6x-Great-Grandfather

DATE	SOURCE	INFORMATION
/ /		Birth
/ /		Baptism
/ /		
/ /		
/ /		
/ /		
/ /		
/ /		
/ /		
/ /		
/ /		
/ /		
/ /		
/ /		
/ /		Death
/ /		Burial

...the child of...

664 Name

7x-Great-Grandfather

DATE	SOURCE	INFORMATION
/ /		Birth
/ /		Baptism
/ /		
/ /		
/ /		
/ /		
/ /		
/ /		
/ /		
/ /		
/ /		Death
/ /		Burial

665 Name

7x-Great-Grandmother

DATE	SOURCE	INFORMATION
/ /		Birth
/ /		Baptism
/ /		
/ /		
/ /		
/ /		
/ /		
/ /		
/ /		
/ /		
/ /		Death
/ /		Burial

6x-Great-Grandmother

Name 333

DATE	SOURCE	INFORMATION
/ /		Birth
/ /		Baptism
/ /		
/ /		
/ /		
/ /		
/ /		
/ /		
/ /		
/ /		
/ /		
/ /		
/ /		
/ /		
/ /		Death
/ /		Burial

...the child of...

666 **Name** 7x-Great-Grandfather

DATE	SOURCE	INFORMATION
/ /		Birth
/ /		Baptism
/ /		
/ /		
/ /		
/ /		
/ /		
/ /		
/ /		
/ /		
/ /		Death
/ /		Burial

667 **Name** 7x-Great-Grandmother

DATE	SOURCE	INFORMATION
/ /		Birth
/ /		Baptism
/ /		
/ /		
/ /		
/ /		
/ /		
/ /		
/ /		
/ /		
/ /		Death
/ /		Burial

334 Name

6x-Great-Grandfather

DATE	SOURCE	INFORMATION
/ /		Birth
/ /		Baptism
/ /		
/ /		
/ /		
/ /		
/ /		
/ /		
/ /		
/ /		
/ /		
/ /		
/ /		
/ /		
/ /		Death
/ /		Burial

...the child of...

668 Name

7x-Great-Grandfather

DATE	SOURCE	INFORMATION
/ /		Birth
/ /		Baptism
/ /		
/ /		
/ /		
/ /		
/ /		
/ /		
/ /		
/ /		
/ /		Death
/ /		Burial

669 Name

7x-Great-Grandmother

DATE	SOURCE	INFORMATION
/ /		Birth
/ /		Baptism
/ /		
/ /		
/ /		
/ /		
/ /		
/ /		
/ /		
/ /		
/ /		Death
/ /		Burial

6x-Great-Grandmother **Name 335**

DATE	SOURCE	INFORMATION
/ /		Birth
/ /		Baptism
/ /		
/ /		
/ /		
/ /		
/ /		
/ /		
/ /		
/ /		
/ /		
/ /		
/ /		
/ /		
/ /		Death
/ /		Burial

...the child of...

670 **Name** 7x-Great-Grandfather

DATE	SOURCE	INFORMATION
/ /		Birth
/ /		Baptism
/ /		
/ /		
/ /		
/ /		
/ /		
/ /		
/ /		
/ /		
/ /		Death
/ /		Burial

671 **Name** 7x-Great-Grandmother

DATE	SOURCE	INFORMATION
/ /		Birth
/ /		Baptism
/ /		
/ /		
/ /		
/ /		
/ /		
/ /		
/ /		
/ /		
/ /		Death
/ /		Burial

336 Name

6x-Great-Grandfather

DATE	SOURCE	INFORMATION
/ /		Birth
/ /		Baptism
/ /		
/ /		
/ /		
/ /		
/ /		
/ /		
/ /		
/ /		
/ /		
/ /		
/ /		
/ /		
/ /		Death
/ /		Burial

...the child of...

672 Name

7x-Great-Grandfather

DATE	SOURCE	INFORMATION
/ /		Birth
/ /		Baptism
/ /		
/ /		
/ /		
/ /		
/ /		
/ /		
/ /		
/ /		
/ /		Death
/ /		Burial

673 Name

7x-Great-Grandmother

DATE	SOURCE	INFORMATION
/ /		Birth
/ /		Baptism
/ /		
/ /		
/ /		
/ /		
/ /		
/ /		
/ /		
/ /		
/ /		Death
/ /		Burial

Name 337

DATE	SOURCE	INFORMATION
/ /		Birth
/ /		Baptism
/ /		
/ /		
/ /		
/ /		
/ /		
/ /		
/ /		
/ /		
/ /		
/ /		
/ /		
/ /		
/ /		Death
/ /		Burial

...the child of...

674 **Name** 7x-Great-Grandfather

DATE	SOURCE	INFORMATION
/ /		Birth
/ /		Baptism
/ /		
/ /		
/ /		
/ /		
/ /		
/ /		
/ /		
/ /		
/ /		Death
/ /		Burial

675 **Name** 7x-Great-Grandmother

DATE	SOURCE	INFORMATION
/ /		Birth
/ /		Baptism
/ /		
/ /		
/ /		
/ /		
/ /		
/ /		
/ /		
/ /		
/ /		Death
/ /		Burial

338 Name

6x-Great-Grandfather

DATE	SOURCE	INFORMATION
/ /		Birth
/ /		Baptism
/ /		
/ /		
/ /		
/ /		
/ /		
/ /		
/ /		
/ /		
/ /		
/ /		
/ /		
/ /		
/ /		Death
/ /		Burial

...the child of...

676 Name

7x-Great-Grandfather

DATE	SOURCE	INFORMATION
/ /		Birth
/ /		Baptism
/ /		
/ /		
/ /		
/ /		
/ /		
/ /		
/ /		
/ /		
/ /		Death
/ /		Burial

677 Name

7x-Great-Grandmother

DATE	SOURCE	INFORMATION
/ /		Birth
/ /		Baptism
/ /		
/ /		
/ /		
/ /		
/ /		
/ /		
/ /		
/ /		
/ /		Death
/ /		Burial

Name 339

DATE	SOURCE	INFORMATION
/ /		Birth
/ /		Baptism
/ /		
/ /		
/ /		
/ /		
/ /		
/ /		
/ /		
/ /		
/ /		
/ /		
/ /		
/ /		
/ /		Death
/ /		Burial

...the child of...

678 **Name** 7x-Great-Grandfather

DATE	SOURCE	INFORMATION
/ /		Birth
/ /		Baptism
/ /		
/ /		
/ /		
/ /		
/ /		
/ /		
/ /		
/ /		
/ /		Death
/ /		Burial

679 **Name** 7x-Great-Grandmother

DATE	SOURCE	INFORMATION
/ /		Birth
/ /		Baptism
/ /		
/ /		
/ /		
/ /		
/ /		
/ /		
/ /		
/ /		
/ /		Death
/ /		Burial

340 Name

6x-Great-Grandfather

DATE	SOURCE	INFORMATION
/ /		Birth
/ /		Baptism
/ /		
/ /		
/ /		
/ /		
/ /		
/ /		
/ /		
/ /		
/ /		
/ /		
/ /		
/ /		
/ /		Death
/ /		Burial

…the child of…

680 Name

7x-Great-Grandfather

DATE	SOURCE	INFORMATION
/ /		Birth
/ /		Baptism
/ /		
/ /		
/ /		
/ /		
/ /		
/ /		
/ /		
/ /		
/ /		Death
/ /		Burial

681 Name

7x-Great-Grandmother

DATE	SOURCE	INFORMATION
/ /		Birth
/ /		Baptism
/ /		
/ /		
/ /		
/ /		
/ /		
/ /		
/ /		
/ /		
/ /		Death
/ /		Burial

6x-Great-Grandmother

Name **341**

DATE	SOURCE	INFORMATION
/ /		Birth
/ /		Baptism
/ /		
/ /		
/ /		
/ /		
/ /		
/ /		
/ /		
/ /		
/ /		
/ /		
/ /		
/ /		
/ /		Death
/ /		Burial

...the child of...

682 **Name** 7x-Great-Grandfather

DATE	SOURCE	INFORMATION
/ /		Birth
/ /		Baptism
/ /		
/ /		
/ /		
/ /		
/ /		
/ /		
/ /		
/ /		
/ /		Death
/ /		Burial

683 **Name** 7x-Great-Grandmother

DATE	SOURCE	INFORMATION
/ /		Birth
/ /		Baptism
/ /		
/ /		
/ /		
/ /		
/ /		
/ /		
/ /		
/ /		
/ /		Death
/ /		Burial

342 Name 6x-Great-Grandfather

DATE	SOURCE	INFORMATION
/ /		Birth
/ /		Baptism
/ /		
/ /		
/ /		
/ /		
/ /		
/ /		
/ /		
/ /		
/ /		
/ /		
/ /		
/ /		
/ /		Death
/ /		Burial

...the child of...

684 Name 7x-Great-Grandfather

DATE	SOURCE	INFORMATION
/ /		Birth
/ /		Baptism
/ /		
/ /		
/ /		
/ /		
/ /		
/ /		
/ /		
/ /		
/ /		Death
/ /		Burial

685 Name 7x-Great-Grandmother

DATE	SOURCE	INFORMATION
/ /		Birth
/ /		Baptism
/ /		
/ /		
/ /		
/ /		
/ /		
/ /		
/ /		
/ /		
/ /		Death
/ /		Burial

6x-Great-Grandmother **Name 343**

DATE	SOURCE	INFORMATION
/ /		Birth
/ /		Baptism
/ /		
/ /		
/ /		
/ /		
/ /		
/ /		
/ /		
/ /		
/ /		
/ /		
/ /		
/ /		
/ /		Death
/ /		Burial

...the child of...

686 **Name** 7x-Great-Grandfather

DATE	SOURCE	INFORMATION
/ /		Birth
/ /		Baptism
/ /		
/ /		
/ /		
/ /		
/ /		
/ /		
/ /		
/ /		
/ /		Death
/ /		Burial

687 **Name** 7x-Great-Grandmother

DATE	SOURCE	INFORMATION
/ /		Birth
/ /		Baptism
/ /		
/ /		
/ /		
/ /		
/ /		
/ /		
/ /		
/ /		
/ /		Death
/ /		Burial

344 Name

6x-Great-Grandfather

DATE	SOURCE	INFORMATION
/ /		Birth
/ /		Baptism
/ /		
/ /		
/ /		
/ /		
/ /		
/ /		
/ /		
/ /		
/ /		
/ /		
/ /		
/ /		
/ /		Death
/ /		Burial

...the child of...

688 Name

7x-Great-Grandfather

DATE	SOURCE	INFORMATION
/ /		Birth
/ /		Baptism
/ /		
/ /		
/ /		
/ /		
/ /		
/ /		
/ /		
/ /		
/ /		Death
/ /		Burial

689 Name

7x-Great-Grandmother

DATE	SOURCE	INFORMATION
/ /		Birth
/ /		Baptism
/ /		
/ /		
/ /		
/ /		
/ /		
/ /		
/ /		
/ /		
/ /		Death
/ /		Burial

Name 345

DATE	SOURCE	INFORMATION
/ /		Birth
/ /		Baptism
/ /		
/ /		
/ /		
/ /		
/ /		
/ /		
/ /		
/ /		
/ /		
/ /		
/ /		
/ /		
/ /		Death
/ /		Burial

...the child of...

690 Name 7x-Great-Grandfather

DATE	SOURCE	INFORMATION
/ /		Birth
/ /		Baptism
/ /		
/ /		
/ /		
/ /		
/ /		
/ /		
/ /		
/ /		
/ /		Death
/ /		Burial

691 Name 7x-Great-Grandmother

DATE	SOURCE	INFORMATION
/ /		Birth
/ /		Baptism
/ /		
/ /		
/ /		
/ /		
/ /		
/ /		
/ /		
/ /		
/ /		Death
/ /		Burial

346 Name

6x-Great-Grandfather

DATE	SOURCE	INFORMATION
/ /		Birth
/ /		Baptism
/ /		
/ /		
/ /		
/ /		
/ /		
/ /		
/ /		
/ /		
/ /		
/ /		
/ /		
/ /		
/ /		Death
/ /		Burial

...the child of...

692 Name

7x-Great-Grandfather

DATE	SOURCE	INFORMATION
/ /		Birth
/ /		Baptism
/ /		
/ /		
/ /		
/ /		
/ /		
/ /		
/ /		
/ /		
/ /		Death
/ /		Burial

693 Name

7x-Great-Grandmother

DATE	SOURCE	INFORMATION
/ /		Birth
/ /		Baptism
/ /		
/ /		
/ /		
/ /		
/ /		
/ /		
/ /		
/ /		
/ /		Death
/ /		Burial

Name 347

DATE	SOURCE	INFORMATION
/ /		Birth
/ /		Baptism
/ /		
/ /		
/ /		
/ /		
/ /		
/ /		
/ /		
/ /		
/ /		
/ /		
/ /		
/ /		
/ /		Death
/ /		Burial

...the child of...

694 **Name** 7x-Great-Grandfather

DATE	SOURCE	INFORMATION
/ /		Birth
/ /		Baptism
/ /		
/ /		
/ /		
/ /		
/ /		
/ /		
/ /		
/ /		
/ /		Death
/ /		Burial

695 **Name** 7x-Great-Grandmother

DATE	SOURCE	INFORMATION
/ /		Birth
/ /		Baptism
/ /		
/ /		
/ /		
/ /		
/ /		
/ /		
/ /		
/ /		
/ /		Death
/ /		Burial

348 **Name**

6x-Great-Grandfather

DATE	SOURCE	INFORMATION
/ /		Birth
/ /		Baptism
/ /		
/ /		
/ /		
/ /		
/ /		
/ /		
/ /		
/ /		
/ /		
/ /		
/ /		
/ /		
/ /		Death
/ /		Burial

...the child of...

696 **Name**

7x-Great-Grandfather

DATE	SOURCE	INFORMATION
/ /		Birth
/ /		Baptism
/ /		
/ /		
/ /		
/ /		
/ /		
/ /		
/ /		
/ /		
/ /		Death
/ /		Burial

697 **Name**

7x-Great-Grandmother

DATE	SOURCE	INFORMATION
/ /		Birth
/ /		Baptism
/ /		
/ /		
/ /		
/ /		
/ /		
/ /		
/ /		
/ /		
/ /		Death
/ /		Burial

6x-Great-Grandmother

Name 349

DATE	SOURCE	INFORMATION
/ /		Birth
/ /		Baptism
/ /		
/ /		
/ /		
/ /		
/ /		
/ /		
/ /		
/ /		
/ /		
/ /		
/ /		
/ /		
/ /		Death
/ /		Burial

...the child of...

698 Name 7x-Great-Grandfather

DATE	SOURCE	INFORMATION
/ /		Birth
/ /		Baptism
/ /		
/ /		
/ /		
/ /		
/ /		
/ /		
/ /		
/ /		
/ /		Death
/ /		Burial

699 Name 7x-Great-Grandmother

DATE	SOURCE	INFORMATION
/ /		Birth
/ /		Baptism
/ /		
/ /		
/ /		
/ /		
/ /		
/ /		
/ /		
/ /		
/ /		Death
/ /		Burial

350 Name

6x-Great-Grandfather

DATE	SOURCE	INFORMATION
/ /		Birth
/ /		Baptism
/ /		
/ /		
/ /		
/ /		
/ /		
/ /		
/ /		
/ /		
/ /		
/ /		
/ /		
/ /		
/ /		Death
/ /		Burial

...the child of...

700 Name

7x-Great-Grandfather

DATE	SOURCE	INFORMATION
/ /		Birth
/ /		Baptism
/ /		
/ /		
/ /		
/ /		
/ /		
/ /		
/ /		
/ /		
/ /		Death
/ /		Burial

701 Name

7x-Great-Grandmother

DATE	SOURCE	INFORMATION
/ /		Birth
/ /		Baptism
/ /		
/ /		
/ /		
/ /		
/ /		
/ /		
/ /		
/ /		
/ /		Death
/ /		Burial

6x-Great-Grandmother

Name 351

DATE	SOURCE	INFORMATION
/ /		Birth
/ /		Baptism
/ /		
/ /		
/ /		
/ /		
/ /		
/ /		
/ /		
/ /		
/ /		
/ /		
/ /		
/ /		
/ /		Death
/ /		Burial

...the child of...

702 **Name** 7x-Great-Grandfather

DATE	SOURCE	INFORMATION
/ /		Birth
/ /		Baptism
/ /		
/ /		
/ /		
/ /		
/ /		
/ /		
/ /		
/ /		
/ /		Death
/ /		Burial

703 **Name** 7x-Great-Grandmother

DATE	SOURCE	INFORMATION
/ /		Birth
/ /		Baptism
/ /		
/ /		
/ /		
/ /		
/ /		
/ /		
/ /		
/ /		
/ /		Death
/ /		Burial

352 Name 6x-Great-Grandfather

DATE	SOURCE	INFORMATION
/ /		Birth
/ /		Baptism
/ /		
/ /		
/ /		
/ /		
/ /		
/ /		
/ /		
/ /		
/ /		
/ /		
/ /		
/ /		
/ /		Death
/ /		Burial

...the child of...

704 Name 7x-Great-Grandfather

DATE	SOURCE	INFORMATION
/ /		Birth
/ /		Baptism
/ /		
/ /		
/ /		
/ /		
/ /		
/ /		
/ /		
/ /		
/ /		Death
/ /		Burial

705 Name 7x-Great-Grandmother

DATE	SOURCE	INFORMATION
/ /		Birth
/ /		Baptism
/ /		
/ /		
/ /		
/ /		
/ /		
/ /		
/ /		
/ /		
/ /		Death
/ /		Burial

Name **353**

DATE	SOURCE	INFORMATION
/ /		Birth
/ /		Baptism
/ /		
/ /		
/ /		
/ /		
/ /		
/ /		
/ /		
/ /		
/ /		
/ /		
/ /		
/ /		
/ /		Death
/ /		Burial

...the child of...

706 Name 7x-Great-Grandfather

DATE	SOURCE	INFORMATION
/ /		Birth
/ /		Baptism
/ /		
/ /		
/ /		
/ /		
/ /		
/ /		
/ /		
/ /		
/ /		Death
/ /		Burial

707 Name 7x-Great-Grandmother

DATE	SOURCE	INFORMATION
/ /		Birth
/ /		Baptism
/ /		
/ /		
/ /		
/ /		
/ /		
/ /		
/ /		
/ /		
/ /		Death
/ /		Burial

354 Name

6x-Great-Grandfather

DATE	SOURCE	INFORMATION
/ /		Birth
/ /		Baptism
/ /		
/ /		
/ /		
/ /		
/ /		
/ /		
/ /		
/ /		
/ /		
/ /		
/ /		
/ /		
/ /		Death
/ /		Burial

...the child of...

708 Name

7x-Great-Grandfather

DATE	SOURCE	INFORMATION
/ /		Birth
/ /		Baptism
/ /		
/ /		
/ /		
/ /		
/ /		
/ /		
/ /		
/ /		
/ /		Death
/ /		Burial

709 Name

7x-Great-Grandmother

DATE	SOURCE	INFORMATION
/ /		Birth
/ /		Baptism
/ /		
/ /		
/ /		
/ /		
/ /		
/ /		
/ /		
/ /		
/ /		Death
/ /		Burial

6x-Great-Grandmother

Name 355

DATE	SOURCE	INFORMATION
/ /		Birth
/ /		Baptism
/ /		
/ /		
/ /		
/ /		
/ /		
/ /		
/ /		
/ /		
/ /		
/ /		
/ /		
/ /		
/ /		Death
/ /		Burial

...the child of...

710 Name 7x-Great-Grandfather

DATE	SOURCE	INFORMATION
/ /		Birth
/ /		Baptism
/ /		
/ /		
/ /		
/ /		
/ /		
/ /		
/ /		
/ /		
/ /		Death
/ /		Burial

711 Name 7x-Great-Grandmother

DATE	SOURCE	INFORMATION
/ /		Birth
/ /		Baptism
/ /		
/ /		
/ /		
/ /		
/ /		
/ /		
/ /		
/ /		
/ /		Death
/ /		Burial

356 Name

6x-Great-Grandfather

DATE	SOURCE	INFORMATION
/ /		Birth
/ /		Baptism
/ /		
/ /		
/ /		
/ /		
/ /		
/ /		
/ /		
/ /		
/ /		
/ /		
/ /		
/ /		
/ /		Death
/ /		Burial

...the child of...

712 Name

7x-Great-Grandfather

DATE	SOURCE	INFORMATION
/ /		Birth
/ /		Baptism
/ /		
/ /		
/ /		
/ /		
/ /		
/ /		
/ /		
/ /		
/ /		Death
/ /		Burial

713 Name

7x-Great-Grandmother

DATE	SOURCE	INFORMATION
/ /		Birth
/ /		Baptism
/ /		
/ /		
/ /		
/ /		
/ /		
/ /		
/ /		
/ /		
/ /		Death
/ /		Burial

Name 357

DATE	SOURCE	INFORMATION
/ /		Birth
/ /		Baptism
/ /		
/ /		
/ /		
/ /		
/ /		
/ /		
/ /		
/ /		
/ /		
/ /		
/ /		
/ /		
/ /		Death
/ /		Burial

...the child of...

714 **Name** 7x-Great-Grandfather

DATE	SOURCE	INFORMATION
/ /		Birth
/ /		Baptism
/ /		
/ /		
/ /		
/ /		
/ /		
/ /		
/ /		
/ /		
/ /		Death
/ /		Burial

715 **Name** 7x-Great-Grandmother

DATE	SOURCE	INFORMATION
/ /		Birth
/ /		Baptism
/ /		
/ /		
/ /		
/ /		
/ /		
/ /		
/ /		
/ /		
/ /		Death
/ /		Burial

358 Name

6x-Great-Grandfather

DATE	SOURCE	INFORMATION
/ /		Birth
/ /		Baptism
/ /		
/ /		
/ /		
/ /		
/ /		
/ /		
/ /		
/ /		
/ /		
/ /		
/ /		
/ /		
/ /		Death
/ /		Burial

...the child of...

716 Name

7x-Great-Grandfather

DATE	SOURCE	INFORMATION
/ /		Birth
/ /		Baptism
/ /		
/ /		
/ /		
/ /		
/ /		
/ /		
/ /		
/ /		
/ /		Death
/ /		Burial

717 Name

7x-Great-Grandmother

DATE	SOURCE	INFORMATION
/ /		Birth
/ /		Baptism
/ /		
/ /		
/ /		
/ /		
/ /		
/ /		
/ /		
/ /		
/ /		Death
/ /		Burial

Name 359

DATE	SOURCE	INFORMATION
/ /		Birth
/ /		Baptism
/ /		
/ /		
/ /		
/ /		
/ /		
/ /		
/ /		
/ /		
/ /		
/ /		
/ /		
/ /		
/ /		Death
/ /		Burial

...the child of...

718 Name 7x-Great-Grandfather

DATE	SOURCE	INFORMATION
/ /		Birth
/ /		Baptism
/ /		
/ /		
/ /		
/ /		
/ /		
/ /		
/ /		
/ /		
/ /		Death
/ /		Burial

719 Name 7x-Great-Grandmother

DATE	SOURCE	INFORMATION
/ /		Birth
/ /		Baptism
/ /		
/ /		
/ /		
/ /		
/ /		
/ /		
/ /		
/ /		
/ /		Death
/ /		Burial

360 Name

6x-Great-Grandfather

DATE	SOURCE	INFORMATION
/ /		Birth
/ /		Baptism
/ /		
/ /		
/ /		
/ /		
/ /		
/ /		
/ /		
/ /		
/ /		
/ /		
/ /		
/ /		
/ /		Death
/ /		Burial

...the child of...

720 Name

7x-Great-Grandfather

DATE	SOURCE	INFORMATION
/ /		Birth
/ /		Baptism
/ /		
/ /		
/ /		
/ /		
/ /		
/ /		
/ /		
/ /		
/ /		Death
/ /		Burial

721 Name

7x-Great-Grandmother

DATE	SOURCE	INFORMATION
/ /		Birth
/ /		Baptism
/ /		
/ /		
/ /		
/ /		
/ /		
/ /		
/ /		
/ /		
/ /		Death
/ /		Burial

Name 361

DATE	SOURCE	INFORMATION
/ /		Birth
/ /		Baptism
/ /		
/ /		
/ /		
/ /		
/ /		
/ /		
/ /		
/ /		
/ /		
/ /		
/ /		
/ /		
/ /		Death
/ /		Burial

...the child of...

722 **Name** 7x-Great-Grandfather

DATE	SOURCE	INFORMATION
/ /		Birth
/ /		Baptism
/ /		
/ /		
/ /		
/ /		
/ /		
/ /		
/ /		
/ /		
/ /		Death
/ /		Burial

723 **Name** 7x-Great-Grandmother

DATE	SOURCE	INFORMATION
/ /		Birth
/ /		Baptism
/ /		
/ /		
/ /		
/ /		
/ /		
/ /		
/ /		
/ /		
/ /		Death
/ /		Burial

362 Name

6x-Great-Grandfather

DATE	SOURCE	INFORMATION
/ /		Birth
/ /		Baptism
/ /		
/ /		
/ /		
/ /		
/ /		
/ /		
/ /		
/ /		
/ /		
/ /		
/ /		
/ /		
/ /		Death
/ /		Burial

...the child of...

724 Name

7x-Great-Grandfather

DATE	SOURCE	INFORMATION
/ /		Birth
/ /		Baptism
/ /		
/ /		
/ /		
/ /		
/ /		
/ /		
/ /		
/ /		
/ /		Death
/ /		Burial

725 Name

7x-Great-Grandmother

DATE	SOURCE	INFORMATION
/ /		Birth
/ /		Baptism
/ /		
/ /		
/ /		
/ /		
/ /		
/ /		
/ /		
/ /		
/ /		Death
/ /		Burial

6x-Great-Grandmother

Name 363

DATE	SOURCE	INFORMATION
/ /		Birth
/ /		Baptism
/ /		
/ /		
/ /		
/ /		
/ /		
/ /		
/ /		
/ /		
/ /		
/ /		
/ /		
/ /		
/ /		Death
/ /		Burial

...the child of...

726 **Name** 7x-Great-Grandfather

DATE	SOURCE	INFORMATION
/ /		Birth
/ /		Baptism
/ /		
/ /		
/ /		
/ /		
/ /		
/ /		
/ /		
/ /		
/ /		Death
/ /		Burial

727 **Name** 7x-Great-Grandmother

DATE	SOURCE	INFORMATION
/ /		Birth
/ /		Baptism
/ /		
/ /		
/ /		
/ /		
/ /		
/ /		
/ /		
/ /		
/ /		Death
/ /		Burial

364 Name

6x-Great-Grandfather

DATE	SOURCE	INFORMATION
/ /		Birth
/ /		Baptism
/ /		
/ /		
/ /		
/ /		
/ /		
/ /		
/ /		
/ /		
/ /		
/ /		
/ /		
/ /		
/ /		Death
/ /		Burial

...the child of...

728 Name

7x-Great-Grandfather

DATE	SOURCE	INFORMATION
/ /		Birth
/ /		Baptism
/ /		
/ /		
/ /		
/ /		
/ /		
/ /		
/ /		
/ /		
/ /		Death
/ /		Burial

729 Name

7x-Great-Grandmother

DATE	SOURCE	INFORMATION
/ /		Birth
/ /		Baptism
/ /		
/ /		
/ /		
/ /		
/ /		
/ /		
/ /		
/ /		
/ /		Death
/ /		Burial

Name 365

DATE	SOURCE	INFORMATION
/ /		Birth
/ /		Baptism
/ /		
/ /		
/ /		
/ /		
/ /		
/ /		
/ /		
/ /		
/ /		
/ /		
/ /		
/ /		
/ /		Death
/ /		Burial

...the child of...

730 **Name** 7x-Great-Grandfather

DATE	SOURCE	INFORMATION
/ /		Birth
/ /		Baptism
/ /		
/ /		
/ /		
/ /		
/ /		
/ /		
/ /		
/ /		
/ /		Death
/ /		Burial

731 **Name** 7x-Great-Grandmother

DATE	SOURCE	INFORMATION
/ /		Birth
/ /		Baptism
/ /		
/ /		
/ /		
/ /		
/ /		
/ /		
/ /		
/ /		
/ /		Death
/ /		Burial

366 Name

6x-Great-Grandfather

DATE	SOURCE	INFORMATION
/ /		Birth
/ /		Baptism
/ /		
/ /		
/ /		
/ /		
/ /		
/ /		
/ /		
/ /		
/ /		
/ /		
/ /		
/ /		
/ /		Death
/ /		Burial

...the child of...

732 Name

7x-Great-Grandfather

DATE	SOURCE	INFORMATION
/ /		Birth
/ /		Baptism
/ /		
/ /		
/ /		
/ /		
/ /		
/ /		
/ /		
/ /		
/ /		Death
/ /		Burial

733 Name

7x-Great-Grandmother

DATE	SOURCE	INFORMATION
/ /		Birth
/ /		Baptism
/ /		
/ /		
/ /		
/ /		
/ /		
/ /		
/ /		
/ /		
/ /		Death
/ /		Burial

Name 367

DATE	SOURCE	INFORMATION
/ /		Birth
/ /		Baptism
/ /		
/ /		
/ /		
/ /		
/ /		
/ /		
/ /		
/ /		
/ /		
/ /		
/ /		
/ /		
/ /		Death
/ /		Burial

...the child of...

734 **Name** 7x-Great-Grandfather

DATE	SOURCE	INFORMATION
/ /		Birth
/ /		Baptism
/ /		
/ /		
/ /		
/ /		
/ /		
/ /		
/ /		
/ /		
/ /		Death
/ /		Burial

735 **Name** 7x-Great-Grandmother

DATE	SOURCE	INFORMATION
/ /		Birth
/ /		Baptism
/ /		
/ /		
/ /		
/ /		
/ /		
/ /		
/ /		
/ /		
/ /		Death
/ /		Burial

368 Name

6x-Great-Grandfather

DATE	SOURCE	INFORMATION
/ /		Birth
/ /		Baptism
/ /		
/ /		
/ /		
/ /		
/ /		
/ /		
/ /		
/ /		
/ /		
/ /		
/ /		
/ /		
/ /		Death
/ /		Burial

...the child of...

736 Name

7x-Great-Grandfather

DATE	SOURCE	INFORMATION
/ /		Birth
/ /		Baptism
/ /		
/ /		
/ /		
/ /		
/ /		
/ /		
/ /		
/ /		
/ /		Death
/ /		Burial

737 Name

7x-Great-Grandmother

DATE	SOURCE	INFORMATION
/ /		Birth
/ /		Baptism
/ /		
/ /		
/ /		
/ /		
/ /		
/ /		
/ /		
/ /		
/ /		Death
/ /		Burial

Name 369

DATE	SOURCE	INFORMATION
/ /		Birth
/ /		Baptism
/ /		
/ /		
/ /		
/ /		
/ /		
/ /		
/ /		
/ /		
/ /		
/ /		
/ /		
/ /		
/ /		Death
/ /		Burial

...the child of...

738 **Name** 7x-Great-Grandfather

DATE	SOURCE	INFORMATION
/ /		Birth
/ /		Baptism
/ /		
/ /		
/ /		
/ /		
/ /		
/ /		
/ /		
/ /		
/ /		Death
/ /		Burial

739 **Name** 7x-Great-Grandmother

DATE	SOURCE	INFORMATION
/ /		Birth
/ /		Baptism
/ /		
/ /		
/ /		
/ /		
/ /		
/ /		
/ /		
/ /		
/ /		Death
/ /		Burial

370 Name

6x-Great-Grandfather

DATE	SOURCE	INFORMATION
/ /		Birth
/ /		Baptism
/ /		
/ /		
/ /		
/ /		
/ /		
/ /		
/ /		
/ /		
/ /		
/ /		
/ /		
/ /		
/ /		Death
/ /		Burial

...the child of...

740 Name

7x-Great-Grandfather

DATE	SOURCE	INFORMATION
/ /		Birth
/ /		Baptism
/ /		
/ /		
/ /		
/ /		
/ /		
/ /		
/ /		
/ /		
/ /		Death
/ /		Burial

741 Name

7x-Great-Grandmother

DATE	SOURCE	INFORMATION
/ /		Birth
/ /		Baptism
/ /		
/ /		
/ /		
/ /		
/ /		
/ /		
/ /		
/ /		
/ /		Death
/ /		Burial

Name 371

DATE	SOURCE	INFORMATION
/ /		Birth
/ /		Baptism
/ /		
/ /		
/ /		
/ /		
/ /		
/ /		
/ /		
/ /		
/ /		
/ /		
/ /		
/ /		
/ /		Death
/ /		Burial

...the child of...

742 Name 7x-Great-Grandfather

DATE	SOURCE	INFORMATION
/ /		Birth
/ /		Baptism
/ /		
/ /		
/ /		
/ /		
/ /		
/ /		
/ /		
/ /		
/ /		Death
/ /		Burial

743 Name 7x-Great-Grandmother

DATE	SOURCE	INFORMATION
/ /		Birth
/ /		Baptism
/ /		
/ /		
/ /		
/ /		
/ /		
/ /		
/ /		
/ /		
/ /		Death
/ /		Burial

372 Name

6x-Great-Grandfather

DATE	SOURCE	INFORMATION
/ /		Birth
/ /		Baptism
/ /		
/ /		
/ /		
/ /		
/ /		
/ /		
/ /		
/ /		
/ /		
/ /		
/ /		
/ /		
/ /		Death
/ /		Burial

...the child of...

744 Name

7x-Great-Grandfather

DATE	SOURCE	INFORMATION
/ /		Birth
/ /		Baptism
/ /		
/ /		
/ /		
/ /		
/ /		
/ /		
/ /		
/ /		
/ /		Death
/ /		Burial

745 Name

7x-Great-Grandmother

DATE	SOURCE	INFORMATION
/ /		Birth
/ /		Baptism
/ /		
/ /		
/ /		
/ /		
/ /		
/ /		
/ /		
/ /		
/ /		Death
/ /		Burial

6x-Great-Grandmother

Name **373**

DATE	SOURCE	INFORMATION
/ /		Birth
/ /		Baptism
/ /		
/ /		
/ /		
/ /		
/ /		
/ /		
/ /		
/ /		
/ /		
/ /		
/ /		
/ /		
/ /		Death
/ /		Burial

...the child of...

746 Name 7x-Great-Grandfather

DATE	SOURCE	INFORMATION
/ /		Birth
/ /		Baptism
/ /		
/ /		
/ /		
/ /		
/ /		
/ /		
/ /		
/ /		
/ /		Death
/ /		Burial

747 Name 7x-Great-Grandmother

DATE	SOURCE	INFORMATION
/ /		Birth
/ /		Baptism
/ /		
/ /		
/ /		
/ /		
/ /		
/ /		
/ /		
/ /		
/ /		Death
/ /		Burial

374 **Name** 6x-Great-Grandfather

DATE	SOURCE	INFORMATION
/ /		Birth
/ /		Baptism
/ /		
/ /		
/ /		
/ /		
/ /		
/ /		
/ /		
/ /		
/ /		
/ /		
/ /		
/ /		
/ /		Death
/ /		Burial

...the child of...

748 **Name** 7x-Great-Grandfather

DATE	SOURCE	INFORMATION
/ /		Birth
/ /		Baptism
/ /		
/ /		
/ /		
/ /		
/ /		
/ /		
/ /		
/ /		
/ /		Death
/ /		Burial

749 **Name** 7x-Great-Grandmother

DATE	SOURCE	INFORMATION
/ /		Birth
/ /		Baptism
/ /		
/ /		
/ /		
/ /		
/ /		
/ /		
/ /		
/ /		
/ /		Death
/ /		Burial

6x-Great-Grandmother

Name 375

DATE	SOURCE	INFORMATION
/ /		Birth
/ /		Baptism
/ /		
/ /		
/ /		
/ /		
/ /		
/ /		
/ /		
/ /		
/ /		
/ /		
/ /		
/ /		
/ /		Death
/ /		Burial

...the child of...

750 **Name** 7x-Great-Grandfather

DATE	SOURCE	INFORMATION
/ /		Birth
/ /		Baptism
/ /		
/ /		
/ /		
/ /		
/ /		
/ /		
/ /		
/ /		
/ /		Death
/ /		Burial

751 **Name** 7x-Great-Grandmother

DATE	SOURCE	INFORMATION
/ /		Birth
/ /		Baptism
/ /		
/ /		
/ /		
/ /		
/ /		
/ /		
/ /		
/ /		
/ /		Death
/ /		Burial

376 Name

6x-Great-Grandfather

DATE	SOURCE	INFORMATION
/ /		Birth
/ /		Baptism
/ /		
/ /		
/ /		
/ /		
/ /		
/ /		
/ /		
/ /		
/ /		
/ /		
/ /		
/ /		
/ /		Death
/ /		Burial

...the child of...

752 Name

7x-Great-Grandfather

DATE	SOURCE	INFORMATION
/ /		Birth
/ /		Baptism
/ /		
/ /		
/ /		
/ /		
/ /		
/ /		
/ /		
/ /		
/ /		Death
/ /		Burial

753 Name

7x-Great-Grandmother

DATE	SOURCE	INFORMATION
/ /		Birth
/ /		Baptism
/ /		
/ /		
/ /		
/ /		
/ /		
/ /		
/ /		
/ /		
/ /		Death
/ /		Burial

Name 377

DATE	SOURCE	INFORMATION
/ /		Birth
/ /		Baptism
/ /		
/ /		
/ /		
/ /		
/ /		
/ /		
/ /		
/ /		
/ /		
/ /		
/ /		
/ /		
/ /		Death
/ /		Burial

...the child of...

754 **Name** 7x-Great-Grandfather

DATE	SOURCE	INFORMATION
/ /		Birth
/ /		Baptism
/ /		
/ /		
/ /		
/ /		
/ /		
/ /		
/ /		
/ /		
/ /		Death
/ /		Burial

755 **Name** 7x-Great-Grandmother

DATE	SOURCE	INFORMATION
/ /		Birth
/ /		Baptism
/ /		
/ /		
/ /		
/ /		
/ /		
/ /		
/ /		
/ /		
/ /		Death
/ /		Burial

378 Name

6x-Great-Grandfather

DATE	SOURCE	INFORMATION
/ /		Birth
/ /		Baptism
/ /		
/ /		
/ /		
/ /		
/ /		
/ /		
/ /		
/ /		
/ /		
/ /		
/ /		
/ /		
/ /		Death
/ /		Burial

...the child of...

756 Name

7x-Great-Grandfather

DATE	SOURCE	INFORMATION
/ /		Birth
/ /		Baptism
/ /		
/ /		
/ /		
/ /		
/ /		
/ /		
/ /		
/ /		
/ /		Death
/ /		Burial

757 Name

7x-Great-Grandmother

DATE	SOURCE	INFORMATION
/ /		Birth
/ /		Baptism
/ /		
/ /		
/ /		
/ /		
/ /		
/ /		
/ /		
/ /		
/ /		Death
/ /		Burial

Name 379

DATE	SOURCE	INFORMATION
/ /		Birth
/ /		Baptism
/ /		
/ /		
/ /		
/ /		
/ /		
/ /		
/ /		
/ /		
/ /		
/ /		
/ /		
/ /		
/ /		Death
/ /		Burial

...the child of...

758 **Name** 7x-Great-Grandfather

DATE	SOURCE	INFORMATION
/ /		Birth
/ /		Baptism
/ /		
/ /		
/ /		
/ /		
/ /		
/ /		
/ /		
/ /		
/ /		Death
/ /		Burial

759 **Name** 7x-Great-Grandmother

DATE	SOURCE	INFORMATION
/ /		Birth
/ /		Baptism
/ /		
/ /		
/ /		
/ /		
/ /		
/ /		
/ /		
/ /		
/ /		Death
/ /		Burial

380 Name

6x-Great-Grandfather

DATE	SOURCE	INFORMATION
/ /		Birth
/ /		Baptism
/ /		
/ /		
/ /		
/ /		
/ /		
/ /		
/ /		
/ /		
/ /		
/ /		
/ /		
/ /		
/ /		Death
/ /		Burial

...the child of...

760 Name

7x-Great-Grandfather

DATE	SOURCE	INFORMATION
/ /		Birth
/ /		Baptism
/ /		
/ /		
/ /		
/ /		
/ /		
/ /		
/ /		
/ /		
/ /		Death
/ /		Burial

761 Name

7x-Great-Grandmother

DATE	SOURCE	INFORMATION
/ /		Birth
/ /		Baptism
/ /		
/ /		
/ /		
/ /		
/ /		
/ /		
/ /		
/ /		
/ /		Death
/ /		Burial

Name 381

DATE	SOURCE	INFORMATION
/ /		Birth
/ /		Baptism
/ /		
/ /		
/ /		
/ /		
/ /		
/ /		
/ /		
/ /		
/ /		
/ /		
/ /		
/ /		
/ /		Death
/ /		Burial

...the child of...

762 **Name** 7x-Great-Grandfather

DATE	SOURCE	INFORMATION
/ /		Birth
/ /		Baptism
/ /		
/ /		
/ /		
/ /		
/ /		
/ /		
/ /		
/ /		
/ /		Death
/ /		Burial

763 **Name** 7x-Great-Grandmother

DATE	SOURCE	INFORMATION
/ /		Birth
/ /		Baptism
/ /		
/ /		
/ /		
/ /		
/ /		
/ /		
/ /		
/ /		
/ /		Death
/ /		Burial

382 Name

6x-Great-Grandfather

DATE	SOURCE	INFORMATION
/ /		Birth
/ /		Baptism
/ /		
/ /		
/ /		
/ /		
/ /		
/ /		
/ /		
/ /		
/ /		
/ /		
/ /		
/ /		
/ /		Death
/ /		Burial

...the child of...

764 Name

7x-Great-Grandfather

DATE	SOURCE	INFORMATION
/ /		Birth
/ /		Baptism
/ /		
/ /		
/ /		
/ /		
/ /		
/ /		
/ /		
/ /		
/ /		Death
/ /		Burial

765 Name

7x-Great-Grandmother

DATE	SOURCE	INFORMATION
/ /		Birth
/ /		Baptism
/ /		
/ /		
/ /		
/ /		
/ /		
/ /		
/ /		
/ /		
/ /		Death
/ /		Burial

Name 383

DATE	SOURCE	INFORMATION
/ /		Birth
/ /		Baptism
/ /		
/ /		
/ /		
/ /		
/ /		
/ /		
/ /		
/ /		
/ /		
/ /		
/ /		
/ /		
/ /		Death
/ /		Burial

...the child of...

766 **Name** 7x-Great-Grandfather

DATE	SOURCE	INFORMATION
/ /		Birth
/ /		Baptism
/ /		
/ /		
/ /		
/ /		
/ /		
/ /		
/ /		
/ /		
/ /		Death
/ /		Burial

767 **Name** 7x-Great-Grandmother

DATE	SOURCE	INFORMATION
/ /		Birth
/ /		Baptism
/ /		
/ /		
/ /		
/ /		
/ /		
/ /		
/ /		
/ /		
/ /		Death
/ /		Burial

384 Name

6x-Great-Grandfather

DATE	SOURCE	INFORMATION
/ /		Birth
/ /		Baptism
/ /		
/ /		
/ /		
/ /		
/ /		
/ /		
/ /		
/ /		
/ /		
/ /		
/ /		
/ /		
/ /		Death
/ /		Burial

...the child of...

768 Name

7x-Great-Grandfather

DATE	SOURCE	INFORMATION
/ /		Birth
/ /		Baptism
/ /		
/ /		
/ /		
/ /		
/ /		
/ /		
/ /		
/ /		
/ /		Death
/ /		Burial

769 Name

7x-Great-Grandmother

DATE	SOURCE	INFORMATION
/ /		Birth
/ /		Baptism
/ /		
/ /		
/ /		
/ /		
/ /		
/ /		
/ /		
/ /		
/ /		Death
/ /		Burial

6x-Great-Grandmother

Name 385

DATE	SOURCE	INFORMATION
/ /		Birth
/ /		Baptism
/ /		
/ /		
/ /		
/ /		
/ /		
/ /		
/ /		
/ /		
/ /		
/ /		
/ /		
/ /		
/ /		Death
/ /		Burial

...the child of...

770 **Name** 7x-Great-Grandfather

DATE	SOURCE	INFORMATION
/ /		Birth
/ /		Baptism
/ /		
/ /		
/ /		
/ /		
/ /		
/ /		
/ /		
/ /		
/ /		Death
/ /		Burial

771 **Name** 7x-Great-Grandmother

DATE	SOURCE	INFORMATION
/ /		Birth
/ /		Baptism
/ /		
/ /		
/ /		
/ /		
/ /		
/ /		
/ /		
/ /		
/ /		Death
/ /		Burial

386 Name

6x-Great-Grandfather

DATE	SOURCE	INFORMATION
/ /		Birth
/ /		Baptism
/ /		
/ /		
/ /		
/ /		
/ /		
/ /		
/ /		
/ /		
/ /		
/ /		
/ /		
/ /		
/ /		Death
/ /		Burial

...the child of...

772 Name

7x-Great-Grandfather

DATE	SOURCE	INFORMATION
/ /		Birth
/ /		Baptism
/ /		
/ /		
/ /		
/ /		
/ /		
/ /		
/ /		
/ /		
/ /		Death
/ /		Burial

773 Name

7x-Great-Grandmother

DATE	SOURCE	INFORMATION
/ /		Birth
/ /		Baptism
/ /		
/ /		
/ /		
/ /		
/ /		
/ /		
/ /		
/ /		
/ /		Death
/ /		Burial

6x-Great-Grandmother **Name 387**

DATE	SOURCE	INFORMATION
/ /		Birth
/ /		Baptism
/ /		
/ /		
/ /		
/ /		
/ /		
/ /		
/ /		
/ /		
/ /		
/ /		
/ /		
/ /		
/ /		Death
/ /		Burial

...the child of...

774 **Name** 7x-Great-Grandfather

DATE	SOURCE	INFORMATION
/ /		Birth
/ /		Baptism
/ /		
/ /		
/ /		
/ /		
/ /		
/ /		
/ /		
/ /		
/ /		Death
/ /		Burial

775 **Name** 7x-Great-Grandmother

DATE	SOURCE	INFORMATION
/ /		Birth
/ /		Baptism
/ /		
/ /		
/ /		
/ /		
/ /		
/ /		
/ /		
/ /		
/ /		Death
/ /		Burial

388 Name

6x-Great-Grandfather

DATE	SOURCE	INFORMATION
/ /		Birth
/ /		Baptism
/ /		
/ /		
/ /		
/ /		
/ /		
/ /		
/ /		
/ /		
/ /		
/ /		
/ /		
/ /		
/ /		Death
/ /		Burial

...the child of...

776 Name

7x-Great-Grandfather

DATE	SOURCE	INFORMATION
/ /		Birth
/ /		Baptism
/ /		
/ /		
/ /		
/ /		
/ /		
/ /		
/ /		
/ /		
/ /		Death
/ /		Burial

777 Name

7x-Great-Grandmother

DATE	SOURCE	INFORMATION
/ /		Birth
/ /		Baptism
/ /		
/ /		
/ /		
/ /		
/ /		
/ /		
/ /		
/ /		
/ /		Death
/ /		Burial

6x-Great-Grandmother

Name 389

DATE	SOURCE	INFORMATION
/ /		Birth
/ /		Baptism
/ /		
/ /		
/ /		
/ /		
/ /		
/ /		
/ /		
/ /		
/ /		
/ /		
/ /		
/ /		
/ /		Death
/ /		Burial

...the child of...

778 **Name** 7x-Great-Grandfather

DATE	SOURCE	INFORMATION
/ /		Birth
/ /		Baptism
/ /		
/ /		
/ /		
/ /		
/ /		
/ /		
/ /		
/ /		
/ /		Death
/ /		Burial

779 **Name** 7x-Great-Grandmother

DATE	SOURCE	INFORMATION
/ /		Birth
/ /		Baptism
/ /		
/ /		
/ /		
/ /		
/ /		
/ /		
/ /		
/ /		
/ /		Death
/ /		Burial

390 Name

6x-GREAT-GRANDFATHER

DATE	SOURCE	INFORMATION
/ /		Birth
/ /		Baptism
/ /		
/ /		
/ /		
/ /		
/ /		
/ /		
/ /		
/ /		
/ /		
/ /		
/ /		
/ /		
/ /		Death
/ /		Burial

...the child of...

780 Name

7x-GREAT-GRANDFATHER

DATE	SOURCE	INFORMATION
/ /		Birth
/ /		Baptism
/ /		
/ /		
/ /		
/ /		
/ /		
/ /		
/ /		
/ /		
/ /		Death
/ /		Burial

781 Name

7x-GREAT-GRANDMOTHER

DATE	SOURCE	INFORMATION
/ /		Birth
/ /		Baptism
/ /		
/ /		
/ /		
/ /		
/ /		
/ /		
/ /		
/ /		
/ /		Death
/ /		Burial

6x-Great-Grandmother

Name 391

DATE	SOURCE	INFORMATION
/ /		Birth
/ /		Baptism
/ /		
/ /		
/ /		
/ /		
/ /		
/ /		
/ /		
/ /		
/ /		
/ /		
/ /		
/ /		
/ /		Death
/ /		Burial

...the child of...

782 **Name** 7x-Great-Grandfather

DATE	SOURCE	INFORMATION
/ /		Birth
/ /		Baptism
/ /		
/ /		
/ /		
/ /		
/ /		
/ /		
/ /		
/ /		
/ /		Death
/ /		Burial

783 **Name** 7x-Great-Grandmother

DATE	SOURCE	INFORMATION
/ /		Birth
/ /		Baptism
/ /		
/ /		
/ /		
/ /		
/ /		
/ /		
/ /		
/ /		
/ /		Death
/ /		Burial

392 Name

6x-Great-Grandfather

DATE	SOURCE	INFORMATION
/ /		Birth
/ /		Baptism
/ /		
/ /		
/ /		
/ /		
/ /		
/ /		
/ /		
/ /		
/ /		
/ /		
/ /		
/ /		
/ /		Death
/ /		Burial

...the child of...

784 Name

7x-Great-Grandfather

DATE	SOURCE	INFORMATION
/ /		Birth
/ /		Baptism
/ /		
/ /		
/ /		
/ /		
/ /		
/ /		
/ /		
/ /		
/ /		Death
/ /		Burial

785 Name

7x-Great-Grandmother

DATE	SOURCE	INFORMATION
/ /		Birth
/ /		Baptism
/ /		
/ /		
/ /		
/ /		
/ /		
/ /		
/ /		
/ /		
/ /		Death
/ /		Burial

Name 393

DATE	SOURCE	INFORMATION
/ /		Birth
/ /		Baptism
/ /		
/ /		
/ /		
/ /		
/ /		
/ /		
/ /		
/ /		
/ /		
/ /		
/ /		
/ /		
/ /		Death
/ /		Burial

...the child of...

786 **Name** 7x-Great-Grandfather

DATE	SOURCE	INFORMATION
/ /		Birth
/ /		Baptism
/ /		
/ /		
/ /		
/ /		
/ /		
/ /		
/ /		
/ /		
/ /		Death
/ /		Burial

787 **Name** 7x-Great-Grandmother

DATE	SOURCE	INFORMATION
/ /		Birth
/ /		Baptism
/ /		
/ /		
/ /		
/ /		
/ /		
/ /		
/ /		
/ /		
/ /		Death
/ /		Burial

394 Name

6x-Great-Grandfather

DATE	SOURCE	INFORMATION
/ /		Birth
/ /		Baptism
/ /		
/ /		
/ /		
/ /		
/ /		
/ /		
/ /		
/ /		
/ /		
/ /		
/ /		
/ /		
/ /		Death
/ /		Burial

...the child of...

788 Name

7x-Great-Grandfather

DATE	SOURCE	INFORMATION
/ /		Birth
/ /		Baptism
/ /		
/ /		
/ /		
/ /		
/ /		
/ /		
/ /		
/ /		
/ /		Death
/ /		Burial

789 Name

7x-Great-Grandmother

DATE	SOURCE	INFORMATION
/ /		Birth
/ /		Baptism
/ /		
/ /		
/ /		
/ /		
/ /		
/ /		
/ /		
/ /		
/ /		Death
/ /		Burial

Name 395

DATE	SOURCE	INFORMATION
/ /		Birth
/ /		Baptism
/ /		
/ /		
/ /		
/ /		
/ /		
/ /		
/ /		
/ /		
/ /		
/ /		
/ /		
/ /		
/ /		Death
/ /		Burial

...the child of...

790 Name 7x-Great-Grandfather

DATE	SOURCE	INFORMATION
/ /		Birth
/ /		Baptism
/ /		
/ /		
/ /		
/ /		
/ /		
/ /		
/ /		
/ /		
/ /		Death
/ /		Burial

791 Name 7x-Great-Grandmother

DATE	SOURCE	INFORMATION
/ /		Birth
/ /		Baptism
/ /		
/ /		
/ /		
/ /		
/ /		
/ /		
/ /		
/ /		
/ /		Death
/ /		Burial

396 Name

6x-Great-Grandfather

DATE	SOURCE	INFORMATION
/ /		Birth
/ /		Baptism
/ /		
/ /		
/ /		
/ /		
/ /		
/ /		
/ /		
/ /		
/ /		
/ /		
/ /		
/ /		
/ /		Death
/ /		Burial

...the child of...

792 Name

7x-Great-Grandfather

DATE	SOURCE	INFORMATION
/ /		Birth
/ /		Baptism
/ /		
/ /		
/ /		
/ /		
/ /		
/ /		
/ /		
/ /		
/ /		Death
/ /		Burial

793 Name

7x-Great-Grandmother

DATE	SOURCE	INFORMATION
/ /		Birth
/ /		Baptism
/ /		
/ /		
/ /		
/ /		
/ /		
/ /		
/ /		
/ /		
/ /		Death
/ /		Burial

Name 397

DATE	SOURCE	INFORMATION
/ /		Birth
/ /		Baptism
/ /		
/ /		
/ /		
/ /		
/ /		
/ /		
/ /		
/ /		
/ /		
/ /		
/ /		
/ /		
/ /		Death
/ /		Burial

...the child of...

794 **Name** 7x-Great-Grandfather

DATE	SOURCE	INFORMATION
/ /		Birth
/ /		Baptism
/ /		
/ /		
/ /		
/ /		
/ /		
/ /		
/ /		
/ /		
/ /		Death
/ /		Burial

795 **Name** 7x-Great-Grandmother

DATE	SOURCE	INFORMATION
/ /		Birth
/ /		Baptism
/ /		
/ /		
/ /		
/ /		
/ /		
/ /		
/ /		
/ /		
/ /		Death
/ /		Burial

398 Name

6x-Great-Grandfather

DATE	SOURCE	INFORMATION
/ /		Birth
/ /		Baptism
/ /		
/ /		
/ /		
/ /		
/ /		
/ /		
/ /		
/ /		
/ /		
/ /		
/ /		
/ /		
/ /		Death
/ /		Burial

...the child of...

796 Name

7x-Great-Grandfather

DATE	SOURCE	INFORMATION
/ /		Birth
/ /		Baptism
/ /		
/ /		
/ /		
/ /		
/ /		
/ /		
/ /		
/ /		
/ /		Death
/ /		Burial

797 Name

7x-Great-Grandmother

DATE	SOURCE	INFORMATION
/ /		Birth
/ /		Baptism
/ /		
/ /		
/ /		
/ /		
/ /		
/ /		
/ /		
/ /		
/ /		Death
/ /		Burial

6x-Great-Grandmother

Name **399**

DATE	SOURCE	INFORMATION
/ /		Birth
/ /		Baptism
/ /		
/ /		
/ /		
/ /		
/ /		
/ /		
/ /		
/ /		
/ /		
/ /		
/ /		
/ /		
/ /		Death
/ /		Burial

...the child of...

798 Name 7x-Great-Grandfather

DATE	SOURCE	INFORMATION
/ /		Birth
/ /		Baptism
/ /		
/ /		
/ /		
/ /		
/ /		
/ /		
/ /		
/ /		
/ /		Death
/ /		Burial

799 Name 7x-Great-Grandmother

DATE	SOURCE	INFORMATION
/ /		Birth
/ /		Baptism
/ /		
/ /		
/ /		
/ /		
/ /		
/ /		
/ /		
/ /		
/ /		Death
/ /		Burial

400 Name

6x-GREAT-GRANDFATHER

DATE	SOURCE	INFORMATION
/ /		Birth
/ /		Baptism
/ /		
/ /		
/ /		
/ /		
/ /		
/ /		
/ /		
/ /		
/ /		
/ /		
/ /		
/ /		
/ /		Death
/ /		Burial

...the child of...

800 Name

7x-GREAT-GRANDFATHER

DATE	SOURCE	INFORMATION
/ /		Birth
/ /		Baptism
/ /		
/ /		
/ /		
/ /		
/ /		
/ /		
/ /		
/ /		
/ /		Death
/ /		Burial

801 Name

7x-GREAT-GRANDMOTHER

DATE	SOURCE	INFORMATION
/ /		Birth
/ /		Baptism
/ /		
/ /		
/ /		
/ /		
/ /		
/ /		
/ /		
/ /		
/ /		Death
/ /		Burial

6x-Great-Grandmother

Name 401

DATE	SOURCE	INFORMATION
/ /		Birth
/ /		Baptism
/ /		
/ /		
/ /		
/ /		
/ /		
/ /		
/ /		
/ /		
/ /		
/ /		
/ /		
/ /		
/ /		Death
/ /		Burial

...the child of...

802 **Name** 7x-Great-Grandfather

DATE	SOURCE	INFORMATION
/ /		Birth
/ /		Baptism
/ /		
/ /		
/ /		
/ /		
/ /		
/ /		
/ /		
/ /		
/ /		Death
/ /		Burial

803 **Name** 7x-Great-Grandmother

DATE	SOURCE	INFORMATION
/ /		Birth
/ /		Baptism
/ /		
/ /		
/ /		
/ /		
/ /		
/ /		
/ /		
/ /		
/ /		Death
/ /		Burial

402 Name

6x-Great-Grandfather

DATE	SOURCE	INFORMATION
/ /		Birth
/ /		Baptism
/ /		
/ /		
/ /		
/ /		
/ /		
/ /		
/ /		
/ /		
/ /		
/ /		
/ /		
/ /		
/ /		Death
/ /		Burial

...the child of...

804 Name

7x-Great-Grandfather

DATE	SOURCE	INFORMATION
/ /		Birth
/ /		Baptism
/ /		
/ /		
/ /		
/ /		
/ /		
/ /		
/ /		
/ /		
/ /		Death
/ /		Burial

805 Name

7x-Great-Grandmother

DATE	SOURCE	INFORMATION
/ /		Birth
/ /		Baptism
/ /		
/ /		
/ /		
/ /		
/ /		
/ /		
/ /		
/ /		
/ /		Death
/ /		Burial

6x-Great-Grandmother

Name 403

DATE	SOURCE	INFORMATION
/ /		Birth
/ /		Baptism
/ /		
/ /		
/ /		
/ /		
/ /		
/ /		
/ /		
/ /		
/ /		
/ /		
/ /		
/ /		
/ /		Death
/ /		Burial

...the child of...

806 **Name** 7x-Great-Grandfather

DATE	SOURCE	INFORMATION
/ /		Birth
/ /		Baptism
/ /		
/ /		
/ /		
/ /		
/ /		
/ /		
/ /		
/ /		
/ /		Death
/ /		Burial

807 **Name** 7x-Great-Grandmother

DATE	SOURCE	INFORMATION
/ /		Birth
/ /		Baptism
/ /		
/ /		
/ /		
/ /		
/ /		
/ /		
/ /		
/ /		
/ /		Death
/ /		Burial

404 Name

6x-Great-Grandfather

DATE	SOURCE	INFORMATION
/ /		Birth
/ /		Baptism
/ /		
/ /		
/ /		
/ /		
/ /		
/ /		
/ /		
/ /		
/ /		
/ /		
/ /		
/ /		
/ /		Death
/ /		Burial

...the child of...

808 Name

7x-Great-Grandfather

DATE	SOURCE	INFORMATION
/ /		Birth
/ /		Baptism
/ /		
/ /		
/ /		
/ /		
/ /		
/ /		
/ /		
/ /		
/ /		Death
/ /		Burial

809 Name

7x-Great-Grandmother

DATE	SOURCE	INFORMATION
/ /		Birth
/ /		Baptism
/ /		
/ /		
/ /		
/ /		
/ /		
/ /		
/ /		
/ /		
/ /		Death
/ /		Burial

6x-Great-Grandmother

Name 405

DATE	SOURCE	INFORMATION
/ /		Birth
/ /		Baptism
/ /		
/ /		
/ /		
/ /		
/ /		
/ /		
/ /		
/ /		
/ /		
/ /		
/ /		
/ /		
/ /		Death
/ /		Burial

...the child of...

810 **Name** 7x-Great-Grandfather

DATE	SOURCE	INFORMATION
/ /		Birth
/ /		Baptism
/ /		
/ /		
/ /		
/ /		
/ /		
/ /		
/ /		
/ /		
/ /		Death
/ /		Burial

811 **Name** 7x-Great-Grandmother

DATE	SOURCE	INFORMATION
/ /		Birth
/ /		Baptism
/ /		
/ /		
/ /		
/ /		
/ /		
/ /		
/ /		
/ /		
/ /		Death
/ /		Burial

406 Name

6x-Great-Grandfather

DATE	SOURCE	INFORMATION
/ /		Birth
/ /		Baptism
/ /		
/ /		
/ /		
/ /		
/ /		
/ /		
/ /		
/ /		
/ /		
/ /		
/ /		
/ /		
/ /		Death
/ /		Burial

...the child of...

812 Name

7x-Great-Grandfather

DATE	SOURCE	INFORMATION
/ /		Birth
/ /		Baptism
/ /		
/ /		
/ /		
/ /		
/ /		
/ /		
/ /		
/ /		
/ /		Death
/ /		Burial

813 Name

7x-Great-Grandmother

DATE	SOURCE	INFORMATION
/ /		Birth
/ /		Baptism
/ /		
/ /		
/ /		
/ /		
/ /		
/ /		
/ /		
/ /		
/ /		Death
/ /		Burial

6x-Great-Grandmother

Name 407

DATE	SOURCE	INFORMATION
/ /		Birth
/ /		Baptism
/ /		
/ /		
/ /		
/ /		
/ /		
/ /		
/ /		
/ /		
/ /		
/ /		
/ /		
/ /		
/ /		Death
/ /		Burial

...the child of...

814 **Name** 7x-Great-Grandfather

DATE	SOURCE	INFORMATION
/ /		Birth
/ /		Baptism
/ /		
/ /		
/ /		
/ /		
/ /		
/ /		
/ /		
/ /		
/ /		Death
/ /		Burial

815 **Name** 7x-Great-Grandmother

DATE	SOURCE	INFORMATION
/ /		Birth
/ /		Baptism
/ /		
/ /		
/ /		
/ /		
/ /		
/ /		
/ /		
/ /		
/ /		Death
/ /		Burial

408 Name

6x-Great-Grandfather

DATE	SOURCE	INFORMATION
/ /		Birth
/ /		Baptism
/ /		
/ /		
/ /		
/ /		
/ /		
/ /		
/ /		
/ /		
/ /		
/ /		
/ /		
/ /		
/ /		Death
/ /		Burial

...the child of...

816 Name

7x-Great-Grandfather

DATE	SOURCE	INFORMATION
/ /		Birth
/ /		Baptism
/ /		
/ /		
/ /		
/ /		
/ /		
/ /		
/ /		
/ /		
/ /		Death
/ /		Burial

817 Name

7x-Great-Grandmother

DATE	SOURCE	INFORMATION
/ /		Birth
/ /		Baptism
/ /		
/ /		
/ /		
/ /		
/ /		
/ /		
/ /		
/ /		
/ /		Death
/ /		Burial

6x-Great-Grandmother

Name 409

DATE	SOURCE	INFORMATION
/ /		Birth
/ /		Baptism
/ /		
/ /		
/ /		
/ /		
/ /		
/ /		
/ /		
/ /		
/ /		
/ /		
/ /		
/ /		
/ /		Death
/ /		Burial

...the child of...

818 **Name** 7x-Great-Grandfather

DATE	SOURCE	INFORMATION
/ /		Birth
/ /		Baptism
/ /		
/ /		
/ /		
/ /		
/ /		
/ /		
/ /		
/ /		
/ /		Death
/ /		Burial

819 **Name** 7x-Great-Grandmother

DATE	SOURCE	INFORMATION
/ /		Birth
/ /		Baptism
/ /		
/ /		
/ /		
/ /		
/ /		
/ /		
/ /		
/ /		
/ /		Death
/ /		Burial

410 Name

6x-Great-Grandfather

DATE	SOURCE	INFORMATION
/ /		Birth
/ /		Baptism
/ /		
/ /		
/ /		
/ /		
/ /		
/ /		
/ /		
/ /		
/ /		
/ /		
/ /		
/ /		
/ /		Death
/ /		Burial

...the child of...

820 Name

7x-Great-Grandfather

DATE	SOURCE	INFORMATION
/ /		Birth
/ /		Baptism
/ /		
/ /		
/ /		
/ /		
/ /		
/ /		
/ /		
/ /		
/ /		Death
/ /		Burial

821 Name

7x-Great-Grandmother

DATE	SOURCE	INFORMATION
/ /		Birth
/ /		Baptism
/ /		
/ /		
/ /		
/ /		
/ /		
/ /		
/ /		
/ /		
/ /		Death
/ /		Burial

Name 411

DATE	SOURCE	INFORMATION
/ /		Birth
/ /		Baptism
/ /		
/ /		
/ /		
/ /		
/ /		
/ /		
/ /		
/ /		
/ /		
/ /		
/ /		
/ /		
/ /		Death
/ /		Burial

...the child of...

822 **Name** 7x-Great-Grandfather

DATE	SOURCE	INFORMATION
/ /		Birth
/ /		Baptism
/ /		
/ /		
/ /		
/ /		
/ /		
/ /		
/ /		
/ /		
/ /		Death
/ /		Burial

823 **Name** 7x-Great-Grandmother

DATE	SOURCE	INFORMATION
/ /		Birth
/ /		Baptism
/ /		
/ /		
/ /		
/ /		
/ /		
/ /		
/ /		
/ /		
/ /		Death
/ /		Burial

412 Name

6x-Great-Grandfather

DATE	SOURCE	INFORMATION
/ /		Birth
/ /		Baptism
/ /		
/ /		
/ /		
/ /		
/ /		
/ /		
/ /		
/ /		
/ /		
/ /		
/ /		
/ /		
/ /		Death
/ /		Burial

...the child of...

824 Name

7x-Great-Grandfather

DATE	SOURCE	INFORMATION
/ /		Birth
/ /		Baptism
/ /		
/ /		
/ /		
/ /		
/ /		
/ /		
/ /		
/ /		
/ /		Death
/ /		Burial

825 Name

7x-Great-Grandmother

DATE	SOURCE	INFORMATION
/ /		Birth
/ /		Baptism
/ /		
/ /		
/ /		
/ /		
/ /		
/ /		
/ /		
/ /		
/ /		Death
/ /		Burial

6x-Great-Grandmother

Name 413

DATE	SOURCE	INFORMATION
/ /		Birth
/ /		Baptism
/ /		
/ /		
/ /		
/ /		
/ /		
/ /		
/ /		
/ /		
/ /		
/ /		
/ /		
/ /		
/ /		Death
/ /		Burial

...the child of...

826 **Name** 7x-Great-Grandfather

DATE	SOURCE	INFORMATION
/ /		Birth
/ /		Baptism
/ /		
/ /		
/ /		
/ /		
/ /		
/ /		
/ /		
/ /		
/ /		Death
/ /		Burial

827 **Name** 7x-Great-Grandmother

DATE	SOURCE	INFORMATION
/ /		Birth
/ /		Baptism
/ /		
/ /		
/ /		
/ /		
/ /		
/ /		
/ /		
/ /		
/ /		Death
/ /		Burial

414 Name

6x-Great-Grandfather

DATE	SOURCE	INFORMATION
/ /		Birth
/ /		Baptism
/ /		
/ /		
/ /		
/ /		
/ /		
/ /		
/ /		
/ /		
/ /		
/ /		
/ /		
/ /		
/ /		Death
/ /		Burial

...the child of...

828 Name

7x-Great-Grandfather

DATE	SOURCE	INFORMATION
/ /		Birth
/ /		Baptism
/ /		
/ /		
/ /		
/ /		
/ /		
/ /		
/ /		
/ /		
/ /		Death
/ /		Burial

829 Name

7x-Great-Grandmother

DATE	SOURCE	INFORMATION
/ /		Birth
/ /		Baptism
/ /		
/ /		
/ /		
/ /		
/ /		
/ /		
/ /		
/ /		
/ /		Death
/ /		Burial

6x-Great-Grandmother **Name 415**

DATE	SOURCE	INFORMATION
/ /		Birth
/ /		Baptism
/ /		
/ /		
/ /		
/ /		
/ /		
/ /		
/ /		
/ /		
/ /		
/ /		
/ /		
/ /		
/ /		Death
/ /		Burial

...the child of...

830 **Name** 7x-Great-Grandfather

DATE	SOURCE	INFORMATION
/ /		Birth
/ /		Baptism
/ /		
/ /		
/ /		
/ /		
/ /		
/ /		
/ /		
/ /		
/ /		Death
/ /		Burial

831 **Name** 7x-Great-Grandmother

DATE	SOURCE	INFORMATION
/ /		Birth
/ /		Baptism
/ /		
/ /		
/ /		
/ /		
/ /		
/ /		
/ /		
/ /		
/ /		Death
/ /		Burial

416 Name

6x-Great-Grandfather

DATE	SOURCE	INFORMATION
/ /		Birth
/ /		Baptism
/ /		
/ /		
/ /		
/ /		
/ /		
/ /		
/ /		
/ /		
/ /		
/ /		
/ /		
/ /		
/ /		Death
/ /		Burial

...the child of...

832 Name

7x-Great-Grandfather

DATE	SOURCE	INFORMATION
/ /		Birth
/ /		Baptism
/ /		
/ /		
/ /		
/ /		
/ /		
/ /		
/ /		
/ /		
/ /		Death
/ /		Burial

833 Name

7x-Great-Grandmother

DATE	SOURCE	INFORMATION
/ /		Birth
/ /		Baptism
/ /		
/ /		
/ /		
/ /		
/ /		
/ /		
/ /		
/ /		
/ /		Death
/ /		Burial

6x-Great-Grandmother

Name 417

DATE	SOURCE	INFORMATION
/ /		Birth
/ /		Baptism
/ /		
/ /		
/ /		
/ /		
/ /		
/ /		
/ /		
/ /		
/ /		
/ /		
/ /		
/ /		
/ /		Death
/ /		Burial

...the child of...

834 **Name** 7x-Great-Grandfather

DATE	SOURCE	INFORMATION
/ /		Birth
/ /		Baptism
/ /		
/ /		
/ /		
/ /		
/ /		
/ /		
/ /		
/ /		
/ /		Death
/ /		Burial

835 **Name** 7x-Great-Grandmother

DATE	SOURCE	INFORMATION
/ /		Birth
/ /		Baptism
/ /		
/ /		
/ /		
/ /		
/ /		
/ /		
/ /		
/ /		
/ /		Death
/ /		Burial

418 Name

6x-Great-Grandfather

DATE	SOURCE	INFORMATION
/ /		Birth
/ /		Baptism
/ /		
/ /		
/ /		
/ /		
/ /		
/ /		
/ /		
/ /		
/ /		
/ /		
/ /		
/ /		
/ /		Death
/ /		Burial

...the child of...

836 Name

7x-Great-Grandfather

DATE	SOURCE	INFORMATION
/ /		Birth
/ /		Baptism
/ /		
/ /		
/ /		
/ /		
/ /		
/ /		
/ /		
/ /		
/ /		Death
/ /		Burial

837 Name

7x-Great-Grandmother

DATE	SOURCE	INFORMATION
/ /		Birth
/ /		Baptism
/ /		
/ /		
/ /		
/ /		
/ /		
/ /		
/ /		
/ /		
/ /		Death
/ /		Burial

Name 419

DATE	SOURCE	INFORMATION
/ /		Birth
/ /		Baptism
/ /		
/ /		
/ /		
/ /		
/ /		
/ /		
/ /		
/ /		
/ /		
/ /		
/ /		
/ /		
/ /		Death
/ /		Burial

...the child of...

838 **Name** 7x-Great-Grandfather

DATE	SOURCE	INFORMATION
/ /		Birth
/ /		Baptism
/ /		
/ /		
/ /		
/ /		
/ /		
/ /		
/ /		
/ /		
/ /		Death
/ /		Burial

839 **Name** 7x-Great-Grandmother

DATE	SOURCE	INFORMATION
/ /		Birth
/ /		Baptism
/ /		
/ /		
/ /		
/ /		
/ /		
/ /		
/ /		
/ /		
/ /		Death
/ /		Burial

420 Name

6x-Great-Grandfather

DATE	SOURCE	INFORMATION
/ /		Birth
/ /		Baptism
/ /		
/ /		
/ /		
/ /		
/ /		
/ /		
/ /		
/ /		
/ /		
/ /		
/ /		
/ /		
/ /		Death
/ /		Burial

...the child of...

840 Name

7x-Great-Grandfather

DATE	SOURCE	INFORMATION
/ /		Birth
/ /		Baptism
/ /		
/ /		
/ /		
/ /		
/ /		
/ /		
/ /		
/ /		
/ /		Death
/ /		Burial

841 Name

7x-Great-Grandmother

DATE	SOURCE	INFORMATION
/ /		Birth
/ /		Baptism
/ /		
/ /		
/ /		
/ /		
/ /		
/ /		
/ /		
/ /		
/ /		Death
/ /		Burial

6x-Great-Grandmother

Name 421

DATE	SOURCE	INFORMATION
/ /		Birth
/ /		Baptism
/ /		
/ /		
/ /		
/ /		
/ /		
/ /		
/ /		
/ /		
/ /		
/ /		
/ /		
/ /		
/ /		Death
/ /		Burial

...the child of...

842 Name 7x-Great-Grandfather

DATE	SOURCE	INFORMATION
/ /		Birth
/ /		Baptism
/ /		
/ /		
/ /		
/ /		
/ /		
/ /		
/ /		
/ /		
/ /		Death
/ /		Burial

843 Name 7x-Great-Grandmother

DATE	SOURCE	INFORMATION
/ /		Birth
/ /		Baptism
/ /		
/ /		
/ /		
/ /		
/ /		
/ /		
/ /		
/ /		
/ /		Death
/ /		Burial

422 Name

6x-GREAT-GRANDFATHER

DATE	SOURCE	INFORMATION
/ /		Birth
/ /		Baptism
/ /		
/ /		
/ /		
/ /		
/ /		
/ /		
/ /		
/ /		
/ /		
/ /		
/ /		
/ /		
/ /		Death
/ /		Burial

...the child of...

844 Name

7x-GREAT-GRANDFATHER

DATE	SOURCE	INFORMATION
/ /		Birth
/ /		Baptism
/ /		
/ /		
/ /		
/ /		
/ /		
/ /		
/ /		
/ /		
/ /		Death
/ /		Burial

845 Name

7x-GREAT-GRANDMOTHER

DATE	SOURCE	INFORMATION
/ /		Birth
/ /		Baptism
/ /		
/ /		
/ /		
/ /		
/ /		
/ /		
/ /		
/ /		
/ /		Death
/ /		Burial

Name 423

DATE	SOURCE	INFORMATION
/ /		Birth
/ /		Baptism
/ /		
/ /		
/ /		
/ /		
/ /		
/ /		
/ /		
/ /		
/ /		
/ /		
/ /		
/ /		
/ /		Death
/ /		Burial

...the child of...

846 **Name** 7X-GREAT-GRANDFATHER

DATE	SOURCE	INFORMATION
/ /		Birth
/ /		Baptism
/ /		
/ /		
/ /		
/ /		
/ /		
/ /		
/ /		
/ /		
/ /		Death
/ /		Burial

847 **Name** 7X-GREAT-GRANDMOTHER

DATE	SOURCE	INFORMATION
/ /		Birth
/ /		Baptism
/ /		
/ /		
/ /		
/ /		
/ /		
/ /		
/ /		
/ /		
/ /		Death
/ /		Burial

424 Name

6x-Great-Grandfather

DATE	SOURCE	INFORMATION
/ /		Birth
/ /		Baptism
/ /		
/ /		
/ /		
/ /		
/ /		
/ /		
/ /		
/ /		
/ /		
/ /		
/ /		
/ /		
/ /		Death
/ /		Burial

...the child of...

848 Name

7x-Great-Grandfather

DATE	SOURCE	INFORMATION
/ /		Birth
/ /		Baptism
/ /		
/ /		
/ /		
/ /		
/ /		
/ /		
/ /		
/ /		
/ /		Death
/ /		Burial

849 Name

7x-Great-Grandmother

DATE	SOURCE	INFORMATION
/ /		Birth
/ /		Baptism
/ /		
/ /		
/ /		
/ /		
/ /		
/ /		
/ /		
/ /		
/ /		Death
/ /		Burial

6x-Great-Grandmother

Name 425

DATE	SOURCE	INFORMATION
/ /		Birth
/ /		Baptism
/ /		
/ /		
/ /		
/ /		
/ /		
/ /		
/ /		
/ /		
/ /		
/ /		
/ /		
/ /		
/ /		Death
/ /		Burial

...the child of...

850 **Name** 7x-Great-Grandfather

DATE	SOURCE	INFORMATION
/ /		Birth
/ /		Baptism
/ /		
/ /		
/ /		
/ /		
/ /		
/ /		
/ /		
/ /		
/ /		Death
/ /		Burial

851 **Name** 7x-Great-Grandmother

DATE	SOURCE	INFORMATION
/ /		Birth
/ /		Baptism
/ /		
/ /		
/ /		
/ /		
/ /		
/ /		
/ /		
/ /		
/ /		Death
/ /		Burial

426 Name

6x-Great-Grandfather

DATE	SOURCE	INFORMATION
/ /		Birth
/ /		Baptism
/ /		
/ /		
/ /		
/ /		
/ /		
/ /		
/ /		
/ /		
/ /		
/ /		
/ /		
/ /		
/ /		Death
/ /		Burial

...the child of...

852 Name

7x-Great-Grandfather

DATE	SOURCE	INFORMATION
/ /		Birth
/ /		Baptism
/ /		
/ /		
/ /		
/ /		
/ /		
/ /		
/ /		
/ /		
/ /		Death
/ /		Burial

853 Name

7x-Great-Grandmother

DATE	SOURCE	INFORMATION
/ /		Birth
/ /		Baptism
/ /		
/ /		
/ /		
/ /		
/ /		
/ /		
/ /		
/ /		
/ /		Death
/ /		Burial

Name 427

DATE	SOURCE	INFORMATION
/ /		Birth
/ /		Baptism
/ /		
/ /		
/ /		
/ /		
/ /		
/ /		
/ /		
/ /		
/ /		
/ /		
/ /		
/ /		
/ /		Death
/ /		Burial

...the child of...

854 Name 7x-Great-Grandfather

DATE	SOURCE	INFORMATION
/ /		Birth
/ /		Baptism
/ /		
/ /		
/ /		
/ /		
/ /		
/ /		
/ /		
/ /		
/ /		Death
/ /		Burial

855 Name 7x-Great-Grandmother

DATE	SOURCE	INFORMATION
/ /		Birth
/ /		Baptism
/ /		
/ /		
/ /		
/ /		
/ /		
/ /		
/ /		
/ /		
/ /		Death
/ /		Burial

428 Name

6x-Great-Grandfather

DATE	SOURCE	INFORMATION
/ /		Birth
/ /		Baptism
/ /		
/ /		
/ /		
/ /		
/ /		
/ /		
/ /		
/ /		
/ /		
/ /		
/ /		
/ /		
/ /		Death
/ /		Burial

...the child of...

856 Name

7x-Great-Grandfather

DATE	SOURCE	INFORMATION
/ /		Birth
/ /		Baptism
/ /		
/ /		
/ /		
/ /		
/ /		
/ /		
/ /		
/ /		
/ /		Death
/ /		Burial

857 Name

7x-Great-Grandmother

DATE	SOURCE	INFORMATION
/ /		Birth
/ /		Baptism
/ /		
/ /		
/ /		
/ /		
/ /		
/ /		
/ /		
/ /		
/ /		Death
/ /		Burial

6x-Great-Grandmother **Name 429**

DATE	SOURCE	INFORMATION
/ /		Birth
/ /		Baptism
/ /		
/ /		
/ /		
/ /		
/ /		
/ /		
/ /		
/ /		
/ /		
/ /		
/ /		
/ /		
/ /		Death
/ /		Burial

...the child of...

858 **Name** 7x-Great-Grandfather

DATE	SOURCE	INFORMATION
/ /		Birth
/ /		Baptism
/ /		
/ /		
/ /		
/ /		
/ /		
/ /		
/ /		
/ /		
/ /		Death
/ /		Burial

859 **Name** 7x-Great-Grandmother

DATE	SOURCE	INFORMATION
/ /		Birth
/ /		Baptism
/ /		
/ /		
/ /		
/ /		
/ /		
/ /		
/ /		
/ /		
/ /		Death
/ /		Burial

430 Name

6x-Great-Grandfather

DATE	SOURCE	INFORMATION
/ /		Birth
/ /		Baptism
/ /		
/ /		
/ /		
/ /		
/ /		
/ /		
/ /		
/ /		
/ /		
/ /		
/ /		
/ /		
/ /		Death
/ /		Burial

...the child of...

860 Name

7x-Great-Grandfather

DATE	SOURCE	INFORMATION
/ /		Birth
/ /		Baptism
/ /		
/ /		
/ /		
/ /		
/ /		
/ /		
/ /		
/ /		
/ /		Death
/ /		Burial

861 Name

7x-Great-Grandmother

DATE	SOURCE	INFORMATION
/ /		Birth
/ /		Baptism
/ /		
/ /		
/ /		
/ /		
/ /		
/ /		
/ /		
/ /		
/ /		Death
/ /		Burial

6x-Great-Grandmother **Name 431**

DATE	SOURCE	INFORMATION
/ /		Birth
/ /		Baptism
/ /		
/ /		
/ /		
/ /		
/ /		
/ /		
/ /		
/ /		
/ /		
/ /		
/ /		
/ /		
/ /		Death
/ /		Burial

...the child of...

862 **Name** 7x-Great-Grandfather

DATE	SOURCE	INFORMATION
/ /		Birth
/ /		Baptism
/ /		
/ /		
/ /		
/ /		
/ /		
/ /		
/ /		
/ /		
/ /		Death
/ /		Burial

863 **Name** 7x-Great-Grandmother

DATE	SOURCE	INFORMATION
/ /		Birth
/ /		Baptism
/ /		
/ /		
/ /		
/ /		
/ /		
/ /		
/ /		
/ /		
/ /		Death
/ /		Burial

432 Name

6x-Great-Grandfather

DATE	SOURCE	INFORMATION
/ /		Birth
/ /		Baptism
/ /		
/ /		
/ /		
/ /		
/ /		
/ /		
/ /		
/ /		
/ /		
/ /		
/ /		
/ /		
/ /		Death
/ /		Burial

...the child of...

864 Name

7x-Great-Grandfather

DATE	SOURCE	INFORMATION
/ /		Birth
/ /		Baptism
/ /		
/ /		
/ /		
/ /		
/ /		
/ /		
/ /		
/ /		
/ /		Death
/ /		Burial

865 Name

7x-Great-Grandmother

DATE	SOURCE	INFORMATION
/ /		Birth
/ /		Baptism
/ /		
/ /		
/ /		
/ /		
/ /		
/ /		
/ /		
/ /		
/ /		Death
/ /		Burial

Name 433

DATE	SOURCE	INFORMATION
/ /		Birth
/ /		Baptism
/ /		
/ /		
/ /		
/ /		
/ /		
/ /		
/ /		
/ /		
/ /		
/ /		
/ /		
/ /		
/ /		Death
/ /		Burial

...the child of...

866 **Name** 7x-Great-Grandfather

DATE	SOURCE	INFORMATION
/ /		Birth
/ /		Baptism
/ /		
/ /		
/ /		
/ /		
/ /		
/ /		
/ /		
/ /		
/ /		Death
/ /		Burial

867 **Name** 7x-Great-Grandmother

DATE	SOURCE	INFORMATION
/ /		Birth
/ /		Baptism
/ /		
/ /		
/ /		
/ /		
/ /		
/ /		
/ /		
/ /		
/ /		Death
/ /		Burial

434 Name

6x-Great-Grandfather

DATE	SOURCE	INFORMATION
/ /		Birth
/ /		Baptism
/ /		
/ /		
/ /		
/ /		
/ /		
/ /		
/ /		
/ /		
/ /		
/ /		
/ /		
/ /		
/ /		Death
/ /		Burial

...the child of...

868 Name

7x-Great-Grandfather

DATE	SOURCE	INFORMATION
/ /		Birth
/ /		Baptism
/ /		
/ /		
/ /		
/ /		
/ /		
/ /		
/ /		
/ /		
/ /		Death
/ /		Burial

869 Name

7x-Great-Grandmother

DATE	SOURCE	INFORMATION
/ /		Birth
/ /		Baptism
/ /		
/ /		
/ /		
/ /		
/ /		
/ /		
/ /		
/ /		
/ /		Death
/ /		Burial

6x-Great-Grandmother **Name 435**

DATE	SOURCE	INFORMATION
/ /		Birth
/ /		Baptism
/ /		
/ /		
/ /		
/ /		
/ /		
/ /		
/ /		
/ /		
/ /		
/ /		
/ /		
/ /		
/ /		Death
/ /		Burial

...the child of...

870 **Name** 7x-Great-Grandfather

DATE	SOURCE	INFORMATION
/ /		Birth
/ /		Baptism
/ /		
/ /		
/ /		
/ /		
/ /		
/ /		
/ /		
/ /		
/ /		Death
/ /		Burial

871 **Name** 7x-Great-Grandmother

DATE	SOURCE	INFORMATION
/ /		Birth
/ /		Baptism
/ /		
/ /		
/ /		
/ /		
/ /		
/ /		
/ /		
/ /		
/ /		Death
/ /		Burial

436 Name

6x-Great-Grandfather

DATE	SOURCE	INFORMATION
/ /		Birth
/ /		Baptism
/ /		
/ /		
/ /		
/ /		
/ /		
/ /		
/ /		
/ /		
/ /		
/ /		
/ /		
/ /		
/ /		Death
/ /		Burial

...the child of...

872 Name

7x-Great-Grandfather

DATE	SOURCE	INFORMATION
/ /		Birth
/ /		Baptism
/ /		
/ /		
/ /		
/ /		
/ /		
/ /		
/ /		
/ /		
/ /		Death
/ /		Burial

873 Name

7x-Great-Grandmother

DATE	SOURCE	INFORMATION
/ /		Birth
/ /		Baptism
/ /		
/ /		
/ /		
/ /		
/ /		
/ /		
/ /		
/ /		
/ /		Death
/ /		Burial

6x-Great-Grandmother

Name 437

DATE	SOURCE	INFORMATION
/ /		Birth
/ /		Baptism
/ /		
/ /		
/ /		
/ /		
/ /		
/ /		
/ /		
/ /		
/ /		
/ /		
/ /		
/ /		
/ /		Death
/ /		Burial

...the child of...

874 **Name** 7x-Great-Grandfather

DATE	SOURCE	INFORMATION
/ /		Birth
/ /		Baptism
/ /		
/ /		
/ /		
/ /		
/ /		
/ /		
/ /		
/ /		
/ /		Death
/ /		Burial

875 **Name** 7x-Great-Grandmother

DATE	SOURCE	INFORMATION
/ /		Birth
/ /		Baptism
/ /		
/ /		
/ /		
/ /		
/ /		
/ /		
/ /		
/ /		
/ /		Death
/ /		Burial

438 Name

6x-Great-Grandfather

DATE	SOURCE	INFORMATION
/ /		Birth
/ /		Baptism
/ /		
/ /		
/ /		
/ /		
/ /		
/ /		
/ /		
/ /		
/ /		
/ /		
/ /		
/ /		
/ /		Death
/ /		Burial

...the child of...

876 Name

7x-Great-Grandfather

DATE	SOURCE	INFORMATION
/ /		Birth
/ /		Baptism
/ /		
/ /		
/ /		
/ /		
/ /		
/ /		
/ /		
/ /		
/ /		Death
/ /		Burial

877 Name

7x-Great-Grandmother

DATE	SOURCE	INFORMATION
/ /		Birth
/ /		Baptism
/ /		
/ /		
/ /		
/ /		
/ /		
/ /		
/ /		
/ /		
/ /		Death
/ /		Burial

6x-Great-Grandmother

Name 439

DATE	SOURCE	INFORMATION
/ /		Birth
/ /		Baptism
/ /		
/ /		
/ /		
/ /		
/ /		
/ /		
/ /		
/ /		
/ /		
/ /		
/ /		
/ /		
/ /		Death
/ /		Burial

...the child of...

878 Name 7x-Great-Grandfather

DATE	SOURCE	INFORMATION
/ /		Birth
/ /		Baptism
/ /		
/ /		
/ /		
/ /		
/ /		
/ /		
/ /		
/ /		
/ /		Death
/ /		Burial

879 Name 7x-Great-Grandmother

DATE	SOURCE	INFORMATION
/ /		Birth
/ /		Baptism
/ /		
/ /		
/ /		
/ /		
/ /		
/ /		
/ /		
/ /		
/ /		Death
/ /		Burial

440 **Name** 6x-Great-Grandfather

DATE	SOURCE	INFORMATION
/ /		Birth
/ /		Baptism
/ /		
/ /		
/ /		
/ /		
/ /		
/ /		
/ /		
/ /		
/ /		
/ /		
/ /		
/ /		
/ /		Death
/ /		Burial

...the child of...

880 **Name** 7x-Great-Grandfather

DATE	SOURCE	INFORMATION
/ /		Birth
/ /		Baptism
/ /		
/ /		
/ /		
/ /		
/ /		
/ /		
/ /		
/ /		
/ /		Death
/ /		Burial

881 **Name** 7x-Great-Grandmother

DATE	SOURCE	INFORMATION
/ /		Birth
/ /		Baptism
/ /		
/ /		
/ /		
/ /		
/ /		
/ /		
/ /		
/ /		
/ /		Death
/ /		Burial

6x-Great-Grandmother

Name 441

DATE	SOURCE	INFORMATION
/ /		Birth
/ /		Baptism
/ /		
/ /		
/ /		
/ /		
/ /		
/ /		
/ /		
/ /		
/ /		
/ /		
/ /		
/ /		
/ /		Death
/ /		Burial

...the child of...

882 **Name** 7x-Great-Grandfather

DATE	SOURCE	INFORMATION
/ /		Birth
/ /		Baptism
/ /		
/ /		
/ /		
/ /		
/ /		
/ /		
/ /		
/ /		
/ /		Death
/ /		Burial

883 **Name** 7x-Great-Grandmother

DATE	SOURCE	INFORMATION
/ /		Birth
/ /		Baptism
/ /		
/ /		
/ /		
/ /		
/ /		
/ /		
/ /		
/ /		
/ /		Death
/ /		Burial

442 Name

6x-Great-Grandfather

DATE	SOURCE	INFORMATION
/ /		Birth
/ /		Baptism
/ /		
/ /		
/ /		
/ /		
/ /		
/ /		
/ /		
/ /		
/ /		
/ /		
/ /		
/ /		
/ /		Death
/ /		Burial

...the child of...

884 Name

7x-Great-Grandfather

DATE	SOURCE	INFORMATION
/ /		Birth
/ /		Baptism
/ /		
/ /		
/ /		
/ /		
/ /		
/ /		
/ /		
/ /		
/ /		Death
/ /		Burial

885 Name

7x-Great-Grandmother

DATE	SOURCE	INFORMATION
/ /		Birth
/ /		Baptism
/ /		
/ /		
/ /		
/ /		
/ /		
/ /		
/ /		
/ /		
/ /		Death
/ /		Burial

6x-Great-Grandmother **Name 443**

DATE	SOURCE	INFORMATION
/ /		Birth
/ /		Baptism
/ /		
/ /		
/ /		
/ /		
/ /		
/ /		
/ /		
/ /		
/ /		
/ /		
/ /		
/ /		
/ /		Death
/ /		Burial

...the child of...

886 **Name** 7x-Great-Grandfather

DATE	SOURCE	INFORMATION
/ /		Birth
/ /		Baptism
/ /		
/ /		
/ /		
/ /		
/ /		
/ /		
/ /		
/ /		
/ /		Death
/ /		Burial

887 **Name** 7x-Great-Grandmother

DATE	SOURCE	INFORMATION
/ /		Birth
/ /		Baptism
/ /		
/ /		
/ /		
/ /		
/ /		
/ /		
/ /		
/ /		
/ /		Death
/ /		Burial

444 **Name**

6x-Great-Grandfather

DATE	SOURCE	INFORMATION
/ /		Birth
/ /		Baptism
/ /		
/ /		
/ /		
/ /		
/ /		
/ /		
/ /		
/ /		
/ /		
/ /		
/ /		
/ /		
/ /		Death
/ /		Burial

...the child of...

888 **Name**

7x-Great-Grandfather

DATE	SOURCE	INFORMATION
/ /		Birth
/ /		Baptism
/ /		
/ /		
/ /		
/ /		
/ /		
/ /		
/ /		
/ /		
/ /		Death
/ /		Burial

889 **Name**

7x-Great-Grandmother

DATE	SOURCE	INFORMATION
/ /		Birth
/ /		Baptism
/ /		
/ /		
/ /		
/ /		
/ /		
/ /		
/ /		
/ /		
/ /		Death
/ /		Burial

Name 445

DATE	SOURCE	INFORMATION
/ /		Birth
/ /		Baptism
/ /		
/ /		
/ /		
/ /		
/ /		
/ /		
/ /		
/ /		
/ /		
/ /		
/ /		
/ /		
/ /		Death
/ /		Burial

...the child of...

890 Name 7x-Great-Grandfather

DATE	SOURCE	INFORMATION
/ /		Birth
/ /		Baptism
/ /		
/ /		
/ /		
/ /		
/ /		
/ /		
/ /		
/ /		
/ /		Death
/ /		Burial

891 Name 7x-Great-Grandmother

DATE	SOURCE	INFORMATION
/ /		Birth
/ /		Baptism
/ /		
/ /		
/ /		
/ /		
/ /		
/ /		
/ /		
/ /		
/ /		Death
/ /		Burial

446 Name

6x-Great-Grandfather

DATE	SOURCE	INFORMATION
/ /		Birth
/ /		Baptism
/ /		
/ /		
/ /		
/ /		
/ /		
/ /		
/ /		
/ /		
/ /		
/ /		
/ /		
/ /		
/ /		Death
/ /		Burial

...the child of...

892 Name

7x-Great-Grandfather

DATE	SOURCE	INFORMATION
/ /		Birth
/ /		Baptism
/ /		
/ /		
/ /		
/ /		
/ /		
/ /		
/ /		
/ /		
/ /		Death
/ /		Burial

893 Name

7x-Great-Grandmother

DATE	SOURCE	INFORMATION
/ /		Birth
/ /		Baptism
/ /		
/ /		
/ /		
/ /		
/ /		
/ /		
/ /		
/ /		
/ /		Death
/ /		Burial

6x-Great-Grandmother

Name **447**

DATE	SOURCE	INFORMATION
/ /		Birth
/ /		Baptism
/ /		
/ /		
/ /		
/ /		
/ /		
/ /		
/ /		
/ /		
/ /		
/ /		
/ /		
/ /		
/ /		Death
/ /		Burial

...the child of...

894 **Name** 7x-Great-Grandfather

DATE	SOURCE	INFORMATION
/ /		Birth
/ /		Baptism
/ /		
/ /		
/ /		
/ /		
/ /		
/ /		
/ /		
/ /		
/ /		Death
/ /		Burial

895 **Name** 7x-Great-Grandmother

DATE	SOURCE	INFORMATION
/ /		Birth
/ /		Baptism
/ /		
/ /		
/ /		
/ /		
/ /		
/ /		
/ /		
/ /		
/ /		Death
/ /		Burial

448 Name

6x-Great-Grandfather

DATE	SOURCE	INFORMATION
/ /		Birth
/ /		Baptism
/ /		
/ /		
/ /		
/ /		
/ /		
/ /		
/ /		
/ /		
/ /		
/ /		
/ /		
/ /		
/ /		Death
/ /		Burial

...the child of...

896 Name

7x-Great-Grandfather

DATE	SOURCE	INFORMATION
/ /		Birth
/ /		Baptism
/ /		
/ /		
/ /		
/ /		
/ /		
/ /		
/ /		
/ /		
/ /		Death
/ /		Burial

897 Name

7x-Great-Grandmother

DATE	SOURCE	INFORMATION
/ /		Birth
/ /		Baptism
/ /		
/ /		
/ /		
/ /		
/ /		
/ /		
/ /		
/ /		
/ /		Death
/ /		Burial

Name 449

DATE	SOURCE	INFORMATION
/ /		Birth
/ /		Baptism
/ /		
/ /		
/ /		
/ /		
/ /		
/ /		
/ /		
/ /		
/ /		
/ /		
/ /		
/ /		
/ /		Death
/ /		Burial

...the child of...

898 Name

7x-Great-Grandfather

DATE	SOURCE	INFORMATION
/ /		Birth
/ /		Baptism
/ /		
/ /		
/ /		
/ /		
/ /		
/ /		
/ /		
/ /		
/ /		Death
/ /		Burial

899 Name

7x-Great-Grandmother

DATE	SOURCE	INFORMATION
/ /		Birth
/ /		Baptism
/ /		
/ /		
/ /		
/ /		
/ /		
/ /		
/ /		
/ /		
/ /		Death
/ /		Burial

450 Name

6x-Great-Grandfather

DATE	SOURCE	INFORMATION
/ /		Birth
/ /		Baptism
/ /		
/ /		
/ /		
/ /		
/ /		
/ /		
/ /		
/ /		
/ /		
/ /		
/ /		
/ /		
/ /		Death
/ /		Burial

...the child of...

900 Name

7x-Great-Grandfather

DATE	SOURCE	INFORMATION
/ /		Birth
/ /		Baptism
/ /		
/ /		
/ /		
/ /		
/ /		
/ /		
/ /		
/ /		
/ /		Death
/ /		Burial

901 Name

7x-Great-Grandmother

DATE	SOURCE	INFORMATION
/ /		Birth
/ /		Baptism
/ /		
/ /		
/ /		
/ /		
/ /		
/ /		
/ /		
/ /		
/ /		Death
/ /		Burial

6x-Great-Grandmother

Name 451

DATE	SOURCE	INFORMATION
/ /		Birth
/ /		Baptism
/ /		
/ /		
/ /		
/ /		
/ /		
/ /		
/ /		
/ /		
/ /		
/ /		
/ /		
/ /		
/ /		Death
/ /		Burial

...the child of...

902 **Name** 7x-Great-Grandfather

DATE	SOURCE	INFORMATION
/ /		Birth
/ /		Baptism
/ /		
/ /		
/ /		
/ /		
/ /		
/ /		
/ /		
/ /		
/ /		Death
/ /		Burial

903 **Name** 7x-Great-Grandmother

DATE	SOURCE	INFORMATION
/ /		Birth
/ /		Baptism
/ /		
/ /		
/ /		
/ /		
/ /		
/ /		
/ /		
/ /		
/ /		Death
/ /		Burial

452 Name

6x-Great-Grandfather

DATE	SOURCE	INFORMATION
/ /		Birth
/ /		Baptism
/ /		
/ /		
/ /		
/ /		
/ /		
/ /		
/ /		
/ /		
/ /		
/ /		
/ /		
/ /		
/ /		Death
/ /		Burial

...the child of...

904 Name

7x-Great-Grandfather

DATE	SOURCE	INFORMATION
/ /		Birth
/ /		Baptism
/ /		
/ /		
/ /		
/ /		
/ /		
/ /		
/ /		
/ /		
/ /		Death
/ /		Burial

905 Name

7x-Great-Grandmother

DATE	SOURCE	INFORMATION
/ /		Birth
/ /		Baptism
/ /		
/ /		
/ /		
/ /		
/ /		
/ /		
/ /		
/ /		
/ /		Death
/ /		Burial

6x-Great-Grandmother **Name 453**

DATE	SOURCE	INFORMATION
/ /		Birth
/ /		Baptism
/ /		
/ /		
/ /		
/ /		
/ /		
/ /		
/ /		
/ /		
/ /		
/ /		
/ /		
/ /		
/ /		Death
/ /		Burial

...the child of...

906 **Name** 7x-Great-Grandfather

DATE	SOURCE	INFORMATION
/ /		Birth
/ /		Baptism
/ /		
/ /		
/ /		
/ /		
/ /		
/ /		
/ /		
/ /		
/ /		Death
/ /		Burial

907 **Name** 7x-Great-Grandmother

DATE	SOURCE	INFORMATION
/ /		Birth
/ /		Baptism
/ /		
/ /		
/ /		
/ /		
/ /		
/ /		
/ /		
/ /		
/ /		Death
/ /		Burial

454 Name

6x-Great-Grandfather

DATE	SOURCE	INFORMATION
/ /		Birth
/ /		Baptism
/ /		
/ /		
/ /		
/ /		
/ /		
/ /		
/ /		
/ /		
/ /		
/ /		
/ /		
/ /		
/ /		Death
/ /		Burial

...the child of...

908 Name

7x-Great-Grandfather

DATE	SOURCE	INFORMATION
/ /		Birth
/ /		Baptism
/ /		
/ /		
/ /		
/ /		
/ /		
/ /		
/ /		
/ /		
/ /		Death
/ /		Burial

909 Name

7x-Great-Grandmother

DATE	SOURCE	INFORMATION
/ /		Birth
/ /		Baptism
/ /		
/ /		
/ /		
/ /		
/ /		
/ /		
/ /		
/ /		
/ /		Death
/ /		Burial

Name 455

DATE	SOURCE	INFORMATION
/ /		Birth
/ /		Baptism
/ /		
/ /		
/ /		
/ /		
/ /		
/ /		
/ /		
/ /		
/ /		
/ /		
/ /		
/ /		
/ /		Death
/ /		Burial

...the child of...

910 **Name** 7x-Great-Grandfather

DATE	SOURCE	INFORMATION
/ /		Birth
/ /		Baptism
/ /		
/ /		
/ /		
/ /		
/ /		
/ /		
/ /		
/ /		
/ /		Death
/ /		Burial

911 **Name** 7x-Great-Grandmother

DATE	SOURCE	INFORMATION
/ /		Birth
/ /		Baptism
/ /		
/ /		
/ /		
/ /		
/ /		
/ /		
/ /		
/ /		
/ /		Death
/ /		Burial

456 Name

6x-Great-Grandfather

DATE	SOURCE	INFORMATION
/ /		Birth
/ /		Baptism
/ /		
/ /		
/ /		
/ /		
/ /		
/ /		
/ /		
/ /		
/ /		
/ /		
/ /		
/ /		
/ /		Death
/ /		Burial

...the child of...

912 Name

7x-Great-Grandfather

DATE	SOURCE	INFORMATION
/ /		Birth
/ /		Baptism
/ /		
/ /		
/ /		
/ /		
/ /		
/ /		
/ /		
/ /		
/ /		Death
/ /		Burial

913 Name

7x-Great-Grandmother

DATE	SOURCE	INFORMATION
/ /		Birth
/ /		Baptism
/ /		
/ /		
/ /		
/ /		
/ /		
/ /		
/ /		
/ /		
/ /		Death
/ /		Burial

6x-Great-Grandmother

Name 457

DATE	SOURCE	INFORMATION
/ /		Birth
/ /		Baptism
/ /		
/ /		
/ /		
/ /		
/ /		
/ /		
/ /		
/ /		
/ /		
/ /		
/ /		
/ /		
/ /		Death
/ /		Burial

...the child of...

914 **Name** 7x-Great-Grandfather

DATE	SOURCE	INFORMATION
/ /		Birth
/ /		Baptism
/ /		
/ /		
/ /		
/ /		
/ /		
/ /		
/ /		
/ /		
/ /		Death
/ /		Burial

915 **Name** 7x-Great-Grandmother

DATE	SOURCE	INFORMATION
/ /		Birth
/ /		Baptism
/ /		
/ /		
/ /		
/ /		
/ /		
/ /		
/ /		
/ /		
/ /		Death
/ /		Burial

458 Name

6x-Great-Grandfather

DATE	SOURCE	INFORMATION
/ /		Birth
/ /		Baptism
/ /		
/ /		
/ /		
/ /		
/ /		
/ /		
/ /		
/ /		
/ /		
/ /		
/ /		
/ /		
/ /		Death
/ /		Burial

...the child of...

916 Name

7x-Great-Grandfather

DATE	SOURCE	INFORMATION
/ /		Birth
/ /		Baptism
/ /		
/ /		
/ /		
/ /		
/ /		
/ /		
/ /		
/ /		
/ /		Death
/ /		Burial

917 Name

7x-Great-Grandmother

DATE	SOURCE	INFORMATION
/ /		Birth
/ /		Baptism
/ /		
/ /		
/ /		
/ /		
/ /		
/ /		
/ /		
/ /		
/ /		Death
/ /		Burial

6X-GREAT-GRANDMOTHER

Name 459

DATE	SOURCE	INFORMATION
/ /		Birth
/ /		Baptism
/ /		
/ /		
/ /		
/ /		
/ /		
/ /		
/ /		
/ /		
/ /		
/ /		
/ /		
/ /		
/ /		Death
/ /		Burial

...the child of...

918 **Name** 7X-GREAT-GRANDFATHER

DATE	SOURCE	INFORMATION
/ /		Birth
/ /		Baptism
/ /		
/ /		
/ /		
/ /		
/ /		
/ /		
/ /		
/ /		
/ /		Death
/ /		Burial

919 **Name** 7X-GREAT-GRANDMOTHER

DATE	SOURCE	INFORMATION
/ /		Birth
/ /		Baptism
/ /		
/ /		
/ /		
/ /		
/ /		
/ /		
/ /		
/ /		
/ /		Death
/ /		Burial

460 Name

6x-Great-Grandfather

DATE	SOURCE	INFORMATION
/ /		Birth
/ /		Baptism
/ /		
/ /		
/ /		
/ /		
/ /		
/ /		
/ /		
/ /		
/ /		
/ /		
/ /		
/ /		
/ /		Death
/ /		Burial

...the child of...

920 Name

7x-Great-Grandfather

DATE	SOURCE	INFORMATION
/ /		Birth
/ /		Baptism
/ /		
/ /		
/ /		
/ /		
/ /		
/ /		
/ /		
/ /		
/ /		Death
/ /		Burial

921 Name

7x-Great-Grandmother

DATE	SOURCE	INFORMATION
/ /		Birth
/ /		Baptism
/ /		
/ /		
/ /		
/ /		
/ /		
/ /		
/ /		
/ /		
/ /		Death
/ /		Burial

6x-Great-Grandmother **Name 461**

DATE	SOURCE	INFORMATION
/ /		Birth
/ /		Baptism
/ /		
/ /		
/ /		
/ /		
/ /		
/ /		
/ /		
/ /		
/ /		
/ /		
/ /		
/ /		
/ /		Death
/ /		Burial

...the child of...

922 **Name** 7x-Great-Grandfather

DATE	SOURCE	INFORMATION
/ /		Birth
/ /		Baptism
/ /		
/ /		
/ /		
/ /		
/ /		
/ /		
/ /		
/ /		
/ /		Death
/ /		Burial

923 **Name** 7x-Great-Grandmother

DATE	SOURCE	INFORMATION
/ /		Birth
/ /		Baptism
/ /		
/ /		
/ /		
/ /		
/ /		
/ /		
/ /		
/ /		
/ /		Death
/ /		Burial

462 Name

6x-Great-Grandfather

DATE	SOURCE	INFORMATION
/ /		Birth
/ /		Baptism
/ /		
/ /		
/ /		
/ /		
/ /		
/ /		
/ /		
/ /		
/ /		
/ /		
/ /		
/ /		
/ /		Death
/ /		Burial

...the child of...

924 Name

7x-Great-Grandfather

DATE	SOURCE	INFORMATION
/ /		Birth
/ /		Baptism
/ /		
/ /		
/ /		
/ /		
/ /		
/ /		
/ /		
/ /		
/ /		Death
/ /		Burial

925 Name

7x-Great-Grandmother

DATE	SOURCE	INFORMATION
/ /		Birth
/ /		Baptism
/ /		
/ /		
/ /		
/ /		
/ /		
/ /		
/ /		
/ /		
/ /		Death
/ /		Burial

6x-Great-Grandmother

Name 463

DATE	SOURCE	INFORMATION
/ /		Birth
/ /		Baptism
/ /		
/ /		
/ /		
/ /		
/ /		
/ /		
/ /		
/ /		
/ /		
/ /		
/ /		
/ /		
/ /		Death
/ /		Burial

...the child of...

926 Name 7x-Great-Grandfather

DATE	SOURCE	INFORMATION
/ /		Birth
/ /		Baptism
/ /		
/ /		
/ /		
/ /		
/ /		
/ /		
/ /		
/ /		
/ /		Death
/ /		Burial

927 Name 7x-Great-Grandmother

DATE	SOURCE	INFORMATION
/ /		Birth
/ /		Baptism
/ /		
/ /		
/ /		
/ /		
/ /		
/ /		
/ /		
/ /		
/ /		Death
/ /		Burial

464 Name

6x-Great-Grandfather

DATE	SOURCE	INFORMATION
/ /		Birth
/ /		Baptism
/ /		
/ /		
/ /		
/ /		
/ /		
/ /		
/ /		
/ /		
/ /		
/ /		
/ /		
/ /		
/ /		Death
/ /		Burial

...the child of...

928 Name

7x-Great-Grandfather

DATE	SOURCE	INFORMATION
/ /		Birth
/ /		Baptism
/ /		
/ /		
/ /		
/ /		
/ /		
/ /		
/ /		
/ /		
/ /		Death
/ /		Burial

929 Name

7x-Great-Grandmother

DATE	SOURCE	INFORMATION
/ /		Birth
/ /		Baptism
/ /		
/ /		
/ /		
/ /		
/ /		
/ /		
/ /		
/ /		
/ /		Death
/ /		Burial

Name 465

DATE	SOURCE	INFORMATION
/ /		Birth
/ /		Baptism
/ /		
/ /		
/ /		
/ /		
/ /		
/ /		
/ /		
/ /		
/ /		
/ /		
/ /		
/ /		
/ /		Death
/ /		Burial

...the child of...

930 **Name** 7x-Great-Grandfather

DATE	SOURCE	INFORMATION
/ /		Birth
/ /		Baptism
/ /		
/ /		
/ /		
/ /		
/ /		
/ /		
/ /		
/ /		
/ /		Death
/ /		Burial

931 **Name** 7x-Great-Grandmother

DATE	SOURCE	INFORMATION
/ /		Birth
/ /		Baptism
/ /		
/ /		
/ /		
/ /		
/ /		
/ /		
/ /		
/ /		
/ /		Death
/ /		Burial

466 Name

6x-Great-Grandfather

DATE	SOURCE	INFORMATION
/ /		Birth
/ /		Baptism
/ /		
/ /		
/ /		
/ /		
/ /		
/ /		
/ /		
/ /		
/ /		
/ /		
/ /		
/ /		
/ /		Death
/ /		Burial

...the child of...

932 Name

7x-Great-Grandfather

DATE	SOURCE	INFORMATION
/ /		Birth
/ /		Baptism
/ /		
/ /		
/ /		
/ /		
/ /		
/ /		
/ /		
/ /		
/ /		Death
/ /		Burial

933 Name

7x-Great-Grandmother

DATE	SOURCE	INFORMATION
/ /		Birth
/ /		Baptism
/ /		
/ /		
/ /		
/ /		
/ /		
/ /		
/ /		
/ /		
/ /		Death
/ /		Burial

Name 467

DATE	SOURCE	INFORMATION
/ /		Birth
/ /		Baptism
/ /		
/ /		
/ /		
/ /		
/ /		
/ /		
/ /		
/ /		
/ /		
/ /		
/ /		
/ /		
/ /		Death
/ /		Burial

...the child of...

934 **Name** 7x-Great-Grandfather

DATE	SOURCE	INFORMATION
/ /		Birth
/ /		Baptism
/ /		
/ /		
/ /		
/ /		
/ /		
/ /		
/ /		
/ /		
/ /		Death
/ /		Burial

935 **Name** 7x-Great-Grandmother

DATE	SOURCE	INFORMATION
/ /		Birth
/ /		Baptism
/ /		
/ /		
/ /		
/ /		
/ /		
/ /		
/ /		
/ /		
/ /		Death
/ /		Burial

468 Name

6x-Great-Grandfather

DATE	SOURCE	INFORMATION
/ /		Birth
/ /		Baptism
/ /		
/ /		
/ /		
/ /		
/ /		
/ /		
/ /		
/ /		
/ /		
/ /		
/ /		
/ /		
/ /		Death
/ /		Burial

...the child of...

936 Name

7x-Great-Grandfather

DATE	SOURCE	INFORMATION
/ /		Birth
/ /		Baptism
/ /		
/ /		
/ /		
/ /		
/ /		
/ /		
/ /		
/ /		
/ /		Death
/ /		Burial

937 Name

7x-Great-Grandmother

DATE	SOURCE	INFORMATION
/ /		Birth
/ /		Baptism
/ /		
/ /		
/ /		
/ /		
/ /		
/ /		
/ /		
/ /		
/ /		Death
/ /		Burial

6x-Great-Grandmother

Name 469

DATE	SOURCE	INFORMATION
/ /		Birth
/ /		Baptism
/ /		
/ /		
/ /		
/ /		
/ /		
/ /		
/ /		
/ /		
/ /		
/ /		
/ /		
/ /		
/ /		Death
/ /		Burial

...the child of...

938 **Name** 7x-Great-Grandfather

DATE	SOURCE	INFORMATION
/ /		Birth
/ /		Baptism
/ /		
/ /		
/ /		
/ /		
/ /		
/ /		
/ /		
/ /		
/ /		Death
/ /		Burial

939 **Name** 7x-Great-Grandmother

DATE	SOURCE	INFORMATION
/ /		Birth
/ /		Baptism
/ /		
/ /		
/ /		
/ /		
/ /		
/ /		
/ /		
/ /		
/ /		Death
/ /		Burial

470 Name

6x-Great-Grandfather

DATE	SOURCE	INFORMATION
/ /		Birth
/ /		Baptism
/ /		
/ /		
/ /		
/ /		
/ /		
/ /		
/ /		
/ /		
/ /		
/ /		
/ /		
/ /		
/ /		Death
/ /		Burial

...the child of...

940 Name

7x-Great-Grandfather

DATE	SOURCE	INFORMATION
/ /		Birth
/ /		Baptism
/ /		
/ /		
/ /		
/ /		
/ /		
/ /		
/ /		
/ /		
/ /		Death
/ /		Burial

941 Name

7x-Great-Grandmother

DATE	SOURCE	INFORMATION
/ /		Birth
/ /		Baptism
/ /		
/ /		
/ /		
/ /		
/ /		
/ /		
/ /		
/ /		
/ /		Death
/ /		Burial

6x-Great-Grandmother

Name 471

DATE	SOURCE	INFORMATION
/ /		Birth
/ /		Baptism
/ /		
/ /		
/ /		
/ /		
/ /		
/ /		
/ /		
/ /		
/ /		
/ /		
/ /		
/ /		
/ /		Death
/ /		Burial

...the child of...

942 **Name** 7x-Great-Grandfather

DATE	SOURCE	INFORMATION
/ /		Birth
/ /		Baptism
/ /		
/ /		
/ /		
/ /		
/ /		
/ /		
/ /		
/ /		
/ /		Death
/ /		Burial

943 **Name** 7x-Great-Grandmother

DATE	SOURCE	INFORMATION
/ /		Birth
/ /		Baptism
/ /		
/ /		
/ /		
/ /		
/ /		
/ /		
/ /		
/ /		
/ /		Death
/ /		Burial

472 Name 6x-Great-Grandfather

DATE	SOURCE	INFORMATION
/ /		Birth
/ /		Baptism
/ /		
/ /		
/ /		
/ /		
/ /		
/ /		
/ /		
/ /		
/ /		
/ /		
/ /		
/ /		
/ /		Death
/ /		Burial

...the child of...

944 Name 7x-Great-Grandfather

DATE	SOURCE	INFORMATION
/ /		Birth
/ /		Baptism
/ /		
/ /		
/ /		
/ /		
/ /		
/ /		
/ /		
/ /		
/ /		Death
/ /		Burial

945 Name 7x-Great-Grandmother

DATE	SOURCE	INFORMATION
/ /		Birth
/ /		Baptism
/ /		
/ /		
/ /		
/ /		
/ /		
/ /		
/ /		
/ /		
/ /		Death
/ /		Burial

6x-Great-Grandmother

Name 473

DATE	SOURCE	INFORMATION
/ /		Birth
/ /		Baptism
/ /		
/ /		
/ /		
/ /		
/ /		
/ /		
/ /		
/ /		
/ /		
/ /		
/ /		
/ /		
/ /		Death
/ /		Burial

...the child of...

946 **Name** 7x-Great-Grandfather

DATE	SOURCE	INFORMATION
/ /		Birth
/ /		Baptism
/ /		
/ /		
/ /		
/ /		
/ /		
/ /		
/ /		
/ /		
/ /		Death
/ /		Burial

947 **Name** 7x-Great-Grandmother

DATE	SOURCE	INFORMATION
/ /		Birth
/ /		Baptism
/ /		
/ /		
/ /		
/ /		
/ /		
/ /		
/ /		
/ /		
/ /		Death
/ /		Burial

474 Name

6x-Great-Grandfather

DATE	SOURCE	INFORMATION
/ /		Birth
/ /		Baptism
/ /		
/ /		
/ /		
/ /		
/ /		
/ /		
/ /		
/ /		
/ /		
/ /		
/ /		
/ /		
/ /		Death
/ /		Burial

...the child of...

948 Name

7x-Great-Grandfather

DATE	SOURCE	INFORMATION
/ /		Birth
/ /		Baptism
/ /		
/ /		
/ /		
/ /		
/ /		
/ /		
/ /		
/ /		
/ /		Death
/ /		Burial

949 Name

7x-Great-Grandmother

DATE	SOURCE	INFORMATION
/ /		Birth
/ /		Baptism
/ /		
/ /		
/ /		
/ /		
/ /		
/ /		
/ /		
/ /		
/ /		Death
/ /		Burial

Name 475

DATE	SOURCE	INFORMATION
/ /		Birth
/ /		Baptism
/ /		
/ /		
/ /		
/ /		
/ /		
/ /		
/ /		
/ /		
/ /		
/ /		
/ /		
/ /		
/ /		Death
/ /		Burial

...the child of...

950 **Name** 7x-Great-Grandfather

DATE	SOURCE	INFORMATION
/ /		Birth
/ /		Baptism
/ /		
/ /		
/ /		
/ /		
/ /		
/ /		
/ /		
/ /		
/ /		Death
/ /		Burial

951 **Name** 7x-Great-Grandmother

DATE	SOURCE	INFORMATION
/ /		Birth
/ /		Baptism
/ /		
/ /		
/ /		
/ /		
/ /		
/ /		
/ /		
/ /		
/ /		Death
/ /		Burial

476 Name

6x-Great-Grandfather

DATE	SOURCE	INFORMATION
/ /		Birth
/ /		Baptism
/ /		
/ /		
/ /		
/ /		
/ /		
/ /		
/ /		
/ /		
/ /		
/ /		
/ /		
/ /		
/ /		Death
/ /		Burial

...the child of...

952 Name

7x-Great-Grandfather

DATE	SOURCE	INFORMATION
/ /		Birth
/ /		Baptism
/ /		
/ /		
/ /		
/ /		
/ /		
/ /		
/ /		
/ /		
/ /		Death
/ /		Burial

953 Name

7x-Great-Grandmother

DATE	SOURCE	INFORMATION
/ /		Birth
/ /		Baptism
/ /		
/ /		
/ /		
/ /		
/ /		
/ /		
/ /		
/ /		
/ /		Death
/ /		Burial

6x-Great-Grandmother **Name 477**

DATE	SOURCE	INFORMATION
/ /		Birth
/ /		Baptism
/ /		
/ /		
/ /		
/ /		
/ /		
/ /		
/ /		
/ /		
/ /		
/ /		
/ /		
/ /		
/ /		Death
/ /		Burial

...the child of...

954 **Name** 7x-Great-Grandfather

DATE	SOURCE	INFORMATION
/ /		Birth
/ /		Baptism
/ /		
/ /		
/ /		
/ /		
/ /		
/ /		
/ /		
/ /		
/ /		Death
/ /		Burial

955 **Name** 7x-Great-Grandmother

DATE	SOURCE	INFORMATION
/ /		Birth
/ /		Baptism
/ /		
/ /		
/ /		
/ /		
/ /		
/ /		
/ /		
/ /		
/ /		Death
/ /		Burial

478 Name

6x-Great-Grandfather

DATE	SOURCE	INFORMATION
/ /		Birth
/ /		Baptism
/ /		
/ /		
/ /		
/ /		
/ /		
/ /		
/ /		
/ /		
/ /		
/ /		
/ /		
/ /		
/ /		Death
/ /		Burial

...the child of...

956 Name

7x-Great-Grandfather

DATE	SOURCE	INFORMATION
/ /		Birth
/ /		Baptism
/ /		
/ /		
/ /		
/ /		
/ /		
/ /		
/ /		
/ /		
/ /		Death
/ /		Burial

957 Name

7x-Great-Grandmother

DATE	SOURCE	INFORMATION
/ /		Birth
/ /		Baptism
/ /		
/ /		
/ /		
/ /		
/ /		
/ /		
/ /		
/ /		
/ /		Death
/ /		Burial

Name 479

DATE	SOURCE	INFORMATION
/ /		Birth
/ /		Baptism
/ /		
/ /		
/ /		
/ /		
/ /		
/ /		
/ /		
/ /		
/ /		
/ /		
/ /		
/ /		
/ /		Death
/ /		Burial

...the child of...

958 **Name** 7X-GREAT-GRANDFATHER

DATE	SOURCE	INFORMATION
/ /		Birth
/ /		Baptism
/ /		
/ /		
/ /		
/ /		
/ /		
/ /		
/ /		
/ /		
/ /		Death
/ /		Burial

959 **Name** 7X-GREAT-GRANDMOTHER

DATE	SOURCE	INFORMATION
/ /		Birth
/ /		Baptism
/ /		
/ /		
/ /		
/ /		
/ /		
/ /		
/ /		
/ /		
/ /		Death
/ /		Burial

480 Name

6x-Great-Grandfather

DATE	SOURCE	INFORMATION
/ /		Birth
/ /		Baptism
/ /		
/ /		
/ /		
/ /		
/ /		
/ /		
/ /		
/ /		
/ /		
/ /		
/ /		
/ /		
/ /		Death
/ /		Burial

...the child of...

960 Name

7x-Great-Grandfather

DATE	SOURCE	INFORMATION
/ /		Birth
/ /		Baptism
/ /		
/ /		
/ /		
/ /		
/ /		
/ /		
/ /		
/ /		
/ /		Death
/ /		Burial

961 Name

7x-Great-Grandmother

DATE	SOURCE	INFORMATION
/ /		Birth
/ /		Baptism
/ /		
/ /		
/ /		
/ /		
/ /		
/ /		
/ /		
/ /		
/ /		Death
/ /		Burial

6x-Great-Grandmother

Name 481

DATE	SOURCE	INFORMATION
/ /		Birth
/ /		Baptism
/ /		
/ /		
/ /		
/ /		
/ /		
/ /		
/ /		
/ /		
/ /		
/ /		
/ /		
/ /		
/ /		Death
/ /		Burial

...the child of...

962 **Name** 7x-Great-Grandfather

DATE	SOURCE	INFORMATION
/ /		Birth
/ /		Baptism
/ /		
/ /		
/ /		
/ /		
/ /		
/ /		
/ /		
/ /		
/ /		Death
/ /		Burial

963 **Name** 7x-Great-Grandmother

DATE	SOURCE	INFORMATION
/ /		Birth
/ /		Baptism
/ /		
/ /		
/ /		
/ /		
/ /		
/ /		
/ /		
/ /		
/ /		Death
/ /		Burial

482 Name

6x-Great-Grandfather

DATE	SOURCE	INFORMATION
/ /		Birth
/ /		Baptism
/ /		
/ /		
/ /		
/ /		
/ /		
/ /		
/ /		
/ /		
/ /		
/ /		
/ /		
/ /		
/ /		Death
/ /		Burial

...the child of...

964 Name

7x-Great-Grandfather

DATE	SOURCE	INFORMATION
/ /		Birth
/ /		Baptism
/ /		
/ /		
/ /		
/ /		
/ /		
/ /		
/ /		
/ /		
/ /		Death
/ /		Burial

965 Name

7x-Great-Grandmother

DATE	SOURCE	INFORMATION
/ /		Birth
/ /		Baptism
/ /		
/ /		
/ /		
/ /		
/ /		
/ /		
/ /		
/ /		
/ /		Death
/ /		Burial

6x-Great-Grandmother

Name 483

DATE	SOURCE	INFORMATION
/ /		Birth
/ /		Baptism
/ /		
/ /		
/ /		
/ /		
/ /		
/ /		
/ /		
/ /		
/ /		
/ /		
/ /		
/ /		
/ /		Death
/ /		Burial

...the child of...

966 **Name** 7x-Great-Grandfather

DATE	SOURCE	INFORMATION
/ /		Birth
/ /		Baptism
/ /		
/ /		
/ /		
/ /		
/ /		
/ /		
/ /		
/ /		
/ /		Death
/ /		Burial

967 **Name** 7x-Great-Grandmother

DATE	SOURCE	INFORMATION
/ /		Birth
/ /		Baptism
/ /		
/ /		
/ /		
/ /		
/ /		
/ /		
/ /		
/ /		
/ /		Death
/ /		Burial

484 Name

6x-Great-Grandfather

DATE	SOURCE	INFORMATION
/ /		Birth
/ /		Baptism
/ /		
/ /		
/ /		
/ /		
/ /		
/ /		
/ /		
/ /		
/ /		
/ /		
/ /		
/ /		
/ /		Death
/ /		Burial

...the child of...

968 Name

7x-Great-Grandfather

DATE	SOURCE	INFORMATION
/ /		Birth
/ /		Baptism
/ /		
/ /		
/ /		
/ /		
/ /		
/ /		
/ /		
/ /		
/ /		Death
/ /		Burial

969 Name

7x-Great-Grandmother

DATE	SOURCE	INFORMATION
/ /		Birth
/ /		Baptism
/ /		
/ /		
/ /		
/ /		
/ /		
/ /		
/ /		
/ /		
/ /		Death
/ /		Burial

6x-Great-Grandmother

Name **485**

DATE	SOURCE	INFORMATION
/ /		Birth
/ /		Baptism
/ /		
/ /		
/ /		
/ /		
/ /		
/ /		
/ /		
/ /		
/ /		
/ /		
/ /		
/ /		
/ /		Death
/ /		Burial

...the child of...

970 Name 7x-Great-Grandfather

DATE	SOURCE	INFORMATION
/ /		Birth
/ /		Baptism
/ /		
/ /		
/ /		
/ /		
/ /		
/ /		
/ /		
/ /		
/ /		Death
/ /		Burial

971 Name 7x-Great-Grandmother

DATE	SOURCE	INFORMATION
/ /		Birth
/ /		Baptism
/ /		
/ /		
/ /		
/ /		
/ /		
/ /		
/ /		
/ /		
/ /		Death
/ /		Burial

486 Name

6x-Great-Grandfather

DATE	SOURCE	INFORMATION
/ /		Birth
/ /		Baptism
/ /		
/ /		
/ /		
/ /		
/ /		
/ /		
/ /		
/ /		
/ /		
/ /		
/ /		
/ /		
/ /		Death
/ /		Burial

...the child of...

972 Name

7x-Great-Grandfather

DATE	SOURCE	INFORMATION
/ /		Birth
/ /		Baptism
/ /		
/ /		
/ /		
/ /		
/ /		
/ /		
/ /		
/ /		
/ /		Death
/ /		Burial

973 Name

7x-Great-Grandmother

DATE	SOURCE	INFORMATION
/ /		Birth
/ /		Baptism
/ /		
/ /		
/ /		
/ /		
/ /		
/ /		
/ /		
/ /		
/ /		Death
/ /		Burial

Name 487

DATE	SOURCE	INFORMATION
/ /		Birth
/ /		Baptism
/ /		
/ /		
/ /		
/ /		
/ /		
/ /		
/ /		
/ /		
/ /		
/ /		
/ /		
/ /		
/ /		Death
/ /		Burial

...the child of...

974 **Name** 7x-Great-Grandfather

DATE	SOURCE	INFORMATION
/ /		Birth
/ /		Baptism
/ /		
/ /		
/ /		
/ /		
/ /		
/ /		
/ /		
/ /		
/ /		Death
/ /		Burial

975 **Name** 7x-Great-Grandmother

DATE	SOURCE	INFORMATION
/ /		Birth
/ /		Baptism
/ /		
/ /		
/ /		
/ /		
/ /		
/ /		
/ /		
/ /		
/ /		Death
/ /		Burial

488 Name 6x-Great-Grandfather

DATE	SOURCE	INFORMATION
/ /		Birth
/ /		Baptism
/ /		
/ /		
/ /		
/ /		
/ /		
/ /		
/ /		
/ /		
/ /		
/ /		
/ /		
/ /		
/ /		Death
/ /		Burial

...the child of...

976 Name 7x-Great-Grandfather

DATE	SOURCE	INFORMATION
/ /		Birth
/ /		Baptism
/ /		
/ /		
/ /		
/ /		
/ /		
/ /		
/ /		
/ /		
/ /		Death
/ /		Burial

977 Name 7x-Great-Grandmother

DATE	SOURCE	INFORMATION
/ /		Birth
/ /		Baptism
/ /		
/ /		
/ /		
/ /		
/ /		
/ /		
/ /		
/ /		
/ /		Death
/ /		Burial

Name 489

DATE	SOURCE	INFORMATION
/ /		Birth
/ /		Baptism
/ /		
/ /		
/ /		
/ /		
/ /		
/ /		
/ /		
/ /		
/ /		
/ /		
/ /		
/ /		
/ /		Death
/ /		Burial

...the child of...

978 **Name** 7x-Great-Grandfather

DATE	SOURCE	INFORMATION
/ /		Birth
/ /		Baptism
/ /		
/ /		
/ /		
/ /		
/ /		
/ /		
/ /		
/ /		
/ /		Death
/ /		Burial

979 **Name** 7x-Great-Grandmother

DATE	SOURCE	INFORMATION
/ /		Birth
/ /		Baptism
/ /		
/ /		
/ /		
/ /		
/ /		
/ /		
/ /		
/ /		
/ /		Death
/ /		Burial

490 Name

6x-Great-Grandfather

DATE	SOURCE	INFORMATION
/ /		Birth
/ /		Baptism
/ /		
/ /		
/ /		
/ /		
/ /		
/ /		
/ /		
/ /		
/ /		
/ /		
/ /		
/ /		
/ /		Death
/ /		Burial

...the child of...

980 Name

7x-Great-Grandfather

DATE	SOURCE	INFORMATION
/ /		Birth
/ /		Baptism
/ /		
/ /		
/ /		
/ /		
/ /		
/ /		
/ /		
/ /		
/ /		Death
/ /		Burial

981 Name

7x-Great-Grandmother

DATE	SOURCE	INFORMATION
/ /		Birth
/ /		Baptism
/ /		
/ /		
/ /		
/ /		
/ /		
/ /		
/ /		
/ /		
/ /		Death
/ /		Burial

6x-Great-Grandmother **Name 491**

DATE	SOURCE	INFORMATION
/ /		Birth
/ /		Baptism
/ /		
/ /		
/ /		
/ /		
/ /		
/ /		
/ /		
/ /		
/ /		
/ /		
/ /		
/ /		
/ /		Death
/ /		Burial

...the child of...

982 **Name** 7x-Great-Grandfather

DATE	SOURCE	INFORMATION
/ /		Birth
/ /		Baptism
/ /		
/ /		
/ /		
/ /		
/ /		
/ /		
/ /		
/ /		
/ /		Death
/ /		Burial

983 **Name** 7x-Great-Grandmother

DATE	SOURCE	INFORMATION
/ /		Birth
/ /		Baptism
/ /		
/ /		
/ /		
/ /		
/ /		
/ /		
/ /		
/ /		
/ /		Death
/ /		Burial

492 Name

6x-Great-Grandfather

DATE	SOURCE	INFORMATION
/ /		Birth
/ /		Baptism
/ /		
/ /		
/ /		
/ /		
/ /		
/ /		
/ /		
/ /		
/ /		
/ /		
/ /		
/ /		
/ /		Death
/ /		Burial

...the child of...

984 Name

7x-Great-Grandfather

DATE	SOURCE	INFORMATION
/ /		Birth
/ /		Baptism
/ /		
/ /		
/ /		
/ /		
/ /		
/ /		
/ /		
/ /		
/ /		Death
/ /		Burial

985 Name

7x-Great-Grandmother

DATE	SOURCE	INFORMATION
/ /		Birth
/ /		Baptism
/ /		
/ /		
/ /		
/ /		
/ /		
/ /		
/ /		
/ /		
/ /		Death
/ /		Burial

Name 493

DATE	SOURCE	INFORMATION
/ /		Birth
/ /		Baptism
/ /		
/ /		
/ /		
/ /		
/ /		
/ /		
/ /		
/ /		
/ /		
/ /		
/ /		
/ /		
/ /		Death
/ /		Burial

...the child of...

986 **Name** 7x-Great-Grandfather

DATE	SOURCE	INFORMATION
/ /		Birth
/ /		Baptism
/ /		
/ /		
/ /		
/ /		
/ /		
/ /		
/ /		
/ /		
/ /		Death
/ /		Burial

987 **Name** 7x-Great-Grandmother

DATE	SOURCE	INFORMATION
/ /		Birth
/ /		Baptism
/ /		
/ /		
/ /		
/ /		
/ /		
/ /		
/ /		
/ /		
/ /		Death
/ /		Burial

494 Name

6x-Great-Grandfather

DATE	SOURCE	INFORMATION
/ /		Birth
/ /		Baptism
/ /		
/ /		
/ /		
/ /		
/ /		
/ /		
/ /		
/ /		
/ /		
/ /		
/ /		
/ /		
/ /		Death
/ /		Burial

...the child of...

988 Name

7x-Great-Grandfather

DATE	SOURCE	INFORMATION
/ /		Birth
/ /		Baptism
/ /		
/ /		
/ /		
/ /		
/ /		
/ /		
/ /		
/ /		
/ /		Death
/ /		Burial

989 Name

7x-Great-Grandmother

DATE	SOURCE	INFORMATION
/ /		Birth
/ /		Baptism
/ /		
/ /		
/ /		
/ /		
/ /		
/ /		
/ /		
/ /		
/ /		Death
/ /		Burial

Name 495

DATE	SOURCE	INFORMATION
/ /		Birth
/ /		Baptism
/ /		
/ /		
/ /		
/ /		
/ /		
/ /		
/ /		
/ /		
/ /		
/ /		
/ /		
/ /		
/ /		Death
/ /		Burial

...the child of...

990 **Name** 7X-GREAT-GRANDFATHER

DATE	SOURCE	INFORMATION
/ /		Birth
/ /		Baptism
/ /		
/ /		
/ /		
/ /		
/ /		
/ /		
/ /		
/ /		
/ /		Death
/ /		Burial

991 **Name** 7X-GREAT-GRANDMOTHER

DATE	SOURCE	INFORMATION
/ /		Birth
/ /		Baptism
/ /		
/ /		
/ /		
/ /		
/ /		
/ /		
/ /		
/ /		
/ /		Death
/ /		Burial

496 Name

6x-Great-Grandfather

DATE	SOURCE	INFORMATION
/ /		Birth
/ /		Baptism
/ /		
/ /		
/ /		
/ /		
/ /		
/ /		
/ /		
/ /		
/ /		
/ /		
/ /		
/ /		
/ /		Death
/ /		Burial

...the child of...

992 Name

7x-Great-Grandfather

DATE	SOURCE	INFORMATION
/ /		Birth
/ /		Baptism
/ /		
/ /		
/ /		
/ /		
/ /		
/ /		
/ /		
/ /		
/ /		Death
/ /		Burial

993 Name

7x-Great-Grandmother

DATE	SOURCE	INFORMATION
/ /		Birth
/ /		Baptism
/ /		
/ /		
/ /		
/ /		
/ /		
/ /		
/ /		
/ /		
/ /		Death
/ /		Burial

6x-Great-Grandmother **Name 497**

DATE	SOURCE	INFORMATION
/ /		Birth
/ /		Baptism
/ /		
/ /		
/ /		
/ /		
/ /		
/ /		
/ /		
/ /		
/ /		
/ /		
/ /		
/ /		
/ /		Death
/ /		Burial

...the child of...

994 **Name** 7x-Great-Grandfather

DATE	SOURCE	INFORMATION
/ /		Birth
/ /		Baptism
/ /		
/ /		
/ /		
/ /		
/ /		
/ /		
/ /		
/ /		
/ /		Death
/ /		Burial

995 **Name** 7x-Great-Grandmother

DATE	SOURCE	INFORMATION
/ /		Birth
/ /		Baptism
/ /		
/ /		
/ /		
/ /		
/ /		
/ /		
/ /		
/ /		
/ /		Death
/ /		Burial

498 Name

6x-Great-Grandfather

DATE	SOURCE	INFORMATION
/ /		Birth
/ /		Baptism
/ /		
/ /		
/ /		
/ /		
/ /		
/ /		
/ /		
/ /		
/ /		
/ /		
/ /		
/ /		
/ /		Death
/ /		Burial

...the child of...

996 Name

7x-Great-Grandfather

DATE	SOURCE	INFORMATION
/ /		Birth
/ /		Baptism
/ /		
/ /		
/ /		
/ /		
/ /		
/ /		
/ /		
/ /		
/ /		Death
/ /		Burial

997 Name

7x-Great-Grandmother

DATE	SOURCE	INFORMATION
/ /		Birth
/ /		Baptism
/ /		
/ /		
/ /		
/ /		
/ /		
/ /		
/ /		
/ /		
/ /		Death
/ /		Burial

6x-Great-Grandmother

Name 499

DATE	SOURCE	INFORMATION
/ /		Birth
/ /		Baptism
/ /		
/ /		
/ /		
/ /		
/ /		
/ /		
/ /		
/ /		
/ /		
/ /		
/ /		
/ /		
/ /		Death
/ /		Burial

...the child of...

998 Name 7x-Great-Grandfather

DATE	SOURCE	INFORMATION
/ /		Birth
/ /		Baptism
/ /		
/ /		
/ /		
/ /		
/ /		
/ /		
/ /		
/ /		
/ /		Death
/ /		Burial

999 Name 7x-Great-Grandmother

DATE	SOURCE	INFORMATION
/ /		Birth
/ /		Baptism
/ /		
/ /		
/ /		
/ /		
/ /		
/ /		
/ /		
/ /		
/ /		Death
/ /		Burial

500 Name
6x-Great-Grandfather

DATE	SOURCE	INFORMATION
/ /		Birth
/ /		Baptism
/ /		
/ /		
/ /		
/ /		
/ /		
/ /		
/ /		
/ /		
/ /		
/ /		
/ /		
/ /		
/ /		Death
/ /		Burial

...the child of...

1000 Name
7x-Great-Grandfather

DATE	SOURCE	INFORMATION
/ /		Birth
/ /		Baptism
/ /		
/ /		
/ /		
/ /		
/ /		
/ /		
/ /		
/ /		
/ /		Death
/ /		Burial

1001 Name
7x-Great-Grandmother

DATE	SOURCE	INFORMATION
/ /		Birth
/ /		Baptism
/ /		
/ /		
/ /		
/ /		
/ /		
/ /		
/ /		
/ /		
/ /		Death
/ /		Burial

6x-Great-Grandmother

Name 501

DATE	SOURCE	INFORMATION
/ /		Birth
/ /		Baptism
/ /		
/ /		
/ /		
/ /		
/ /		
/ /		
/ /		
/ /		
/ /		
/ /		
/ /		
/ /		
/ /		Death
/ /		Burial

...the child of...

1002 Name 7x-Great-Grandfather

DATE	SOURCE	INFORMATION
/ /		Birth
/ /		Baptism
/ /		
/ /		
/ /		
/ /		
/ /		
/ /		
/ /		
/ /		
/ /		Death
/ /		Burial

1003 Name 7x-Great-Grandmother

DATE	SOURCE	INFORMATION
/ /		Birth
/ /		Baptism
/ /		
/ /		
/ /		
/ /		
/ /		
/ /		
/ /		
/ /		
/ /		Death
/ /		Burial

502 Name

6x-GREAT-GRANDFATHER

DATE	SOURCE	INFORMATION
/ /		Birth
/ /		Baptism
/ /		
/ /		
/ /		
/ /		
/ /		
/ /		
/ /		
/ /		
/ /		
/ /		
/ /		
/ /		
/ /		Death
/ /		Burial

...the child of...

1004 Name

7x-GREAT-GRANDFATHER

DATE	SOURCE	INFORMATION
/ /		Birth
/ /		Baptism
/ /		
/ /		
/ /		
/ /		
/ /		
/ /		
/ /		
/ /		
/ /		Death
/ /		Burial

1005 Name

7x-GREAT-GRANDMOTHER

DATE	SOURCE	INFORMATION
/ /		Birth
/ /		Baptism
/ /		
/ /		
/ /		
/ /		
/ /		
/ /		
/ /		
/ /		
/ /		Death
/ /		Burial

6x-Great-Grandmother

Name 503

DATE	SOURCE	INFORMATION
/ /		Birth
/ /		Baptism
/ /		
/ /		
/ /		
/ /		
/ /		
/ /		
/ /		
/ /		
/ /		
/ /		
/ /		
/ /		
/ /		Death
/ /		Burial

...the child of...

1006 Name 7x-Great-Grandfather

DATE	SOURCE	INFORMATION
/ /		Birth
/ /		Baptism
/ /		
/ /		
/ /		
/ /		
/ /		
/ /		
/ /		
/ /		
/ /		Death
/ /		Burial

1007 Name 7x-Great-Grandmother

DATE	SOURCE	INFORMATION
/ /		Birth
/ /		Baptism
/ /		
/ /		
/ /		
/ /		
/ /		
/ /		
/ /		
/ /		
/ /		Death
/ /		Burial

504 Name

6x-Great-Grandfather

DATE	SOURCE	INFORMATION
/ /		Birth
/ /		Baptism
/ /		
/ /		
/ /		
/ /		
/ /		
/ /		
/ /		
/ /		
/ /		
/ /		
/ /		
/ /		
/ /		Death
/ /		Burial

...the child of...

1008 Name

7x-Great-Grandfather

DATE	SOURCE	INFORMATION
/ /		Birth
/ /		Baptism
/ /		
/ /		
/ /		
/ /		
/ /		
/ /		
/ /		
/ /		
/ /		Death
/ /		Burial

1009 Name

7x-Great-Grandmother

DATE	SOURCE	INFORMATION
/ /		Birth
/ /		Baptism
/ /		
/ /		
/ /		
/ /		
/ /		
/ /		
/ /		
/ /		
/ /		Death
/ /		Burial

6x-Great-Grandmother **Name 505**

DATE	SOURCE	INFORMATION
/ /		Birth
/ /		Baptism
/ /		
/ /		
/ /		
/ /		
/ /		
/ /		
/ /		
/ /		
/ /		
/ /		
/ /		
/ /		
/ /		Death
/ /		Burial

...the child of...

1010 Name 7x-Great-Grandfather

DATE	SOURCE	INFORMATION
/ /		Birth
/ /		Baptism
/ /		
/ /		
/ /		
/ /		
/ /		
/ /		
/ /		
/ /		
/ /		Death
/ /		Burial

1011 Name 7x-Great-Grandmother

DATE	SOURCE	INFORMATION
/ /		Birth
/ /		Baptism
/ /		
/ /		
/ /		
/ /		
/ /		
/ /		
/ /		
/ /		
/ /		Death
/ /		Burial

506 Name

6x-GREAT-GRANDFATHER

DATE	SOURCE	INFORMATION
/ /		Birth
/ /		Baptism
/ /		
/ /		
/ /		
/ /		
/ /		
/ /		
/ /		
/ /		
/ /		
/ /		
/ /		
/ /		
/ /		Death
/ /		Burial

...the child of...

1012 Name

7x-GREAT-GRANDFATHER

DATE	SOURCE	INFORMATION
/ /		Birth
/ /		Baptism
/ /		
/ /		
/ /		
/ /		
/ /		
/ /		
/ /		
/ /		
/ /		Death
/ /		Burial

1013 Name

7x-GREAT-GRANDMOTHER

DATE	SOURCE	INFORMATION
/ /		Birth
/ /		Baptism
/ /		
/ /		
/ /		
/ /		
/ /		
/ /		
/ /		
/ /		
/ /		Death
/ /		Burial

6x-Great-Grandmother

Name 507

DATE	SOURCE	INFORMATION
/ /		Birth
/ /		Baptism
/ /		
/ /		
/ /		
/ /		
/ /		
/ /		
/ /		
/ /		
/ /		
/ /		
/ /		
/ /		
/ /		Death
/ /		Burial

...the child of...

1014 Name 7x-Great-Grandfather

DATE	SOURCE	INFORMATION
/ /		Birth
/ /		Baptism
/ /		
/ /		
/ /		
/ /		
/ /		
/ /		
/ /		
/ /		
/ /		Death
/ /		Burial

1015 Name 7x-Great-Grandmother

DATE	SOURCE	INFORMATION
/ /		Birth
/ /		Baptism
/ /		
/ /		
/ /		
/ /		
/ /		
/ /		
/ /		
/ /		
/ /		Death
/ /		Burial

508 Name

6x-Great-Grandfather

DATE	SOURCE	INFORMATION
/ /		Birth
/ /		Baptism
/ /		
/ /		
/ /		
/ /		
/ /		
/ /		
/ /		
/ /		
/ /		
/ /		
/ /		
/ /		
/ /		Death
/ /		Burial

...the child of...

1016 Name

7x-Great-Grandfather

DATE	SOURCE	INFORMATION
/ /		Birth
/ /		Baptism
/ /		
/ /		
/ /		
/ /		
/ /		
/ /		
/ /		
/ /		
/ /		Death
/ /		Burial

1017 Name

7x-Great-Grandmother

DATE	SOURCE	INFORMATION
/ /		Birth
/ /		Baptism
/ /		
/ /		
/ /		
/ /		
/ /		
/ /		
/ /		
/ /		
/ /		Death
/ /		Burial

Name 509

DATE	SOURCE	INFORMATION
/ /		Birth
/ /		Baptism
/ /		
/ /		
/ /		
/ /		
/ /		
/ /		
/ /		
/ /		
/ /		
/ /		
/ /		
/ /		
/ /		Death
/ /		Burial

...the child of...

1018 **Name** 7x-Great-Grandfather

DATE	SOURCE	INFORMATION
/ /		Birth
/ /		Baptism
/ /		
/ /		
/ /		
/ /		
/ /		
/ /		
/ /		
/ /		
/ /		Death
/ /		Burial

1019 **Name** 7x-Great-Grandmother

DATE	SOURCE	INFORMATION
/ /		Birth
/ /		Baptism
/ /		
/ /		
/ /		
/ /		
/ /		
/ /		
/ /		
/ /		
/ /		Death
/ /		Burial

510 Name

6x-GREAT-GRANDFATHER

DATE	SOURCE	INFORMATION
/ /		Birth
/ /		Baptism
/ /		
/ /		
/ /		
/ /		
/ /		
/ /		
/ /		
/ /		
/ /		
/ /		
/ /		
/ /		
/ /		Death
/ /		Burial

...the child of...

1020 Name

7x-GREAT-GRANDFATHER

DATE	SOURCE	INFORMATION
/ /		Birth
/ /		Baptism
/ /		
/ /		
/ /		
/ /		
/ /		
/ /		
/ /		
/ /		
/ /		Death
/ /		Burial

1021 Name

7x-GREAT-GRANDMOTHER

DATE	SOURCE	INFORMATION
/ /		Birth
/ /		Baptism
/ /		
/ /		
/ /		
/ /		
/ /		
/ /		
/ /		
/ /		
/ /		Death
/ /		Burial

Name **511**

DATE	SOURCE	INFORMATION
/ /		Birth
/ /		Baptism
/ /		
/ /		
/ /		
/ /		
/ /		
/ /		
/ /		
/ /		
/ /		
/ /		
/ /		
/ /		
/ /		Death
/ /		Burial

...the child of...

1022 Name 7x-Great-Grandfather

DATE	SOURCE	INFORMATION
/ /		Birth
/ /		Baptism
/ /		
/ /		
/ /		
/ /		
/ /		
/ /		
/ /		
/ /		
/ /		Death
/ /		Burial

1023 Name 7x-Great-Grandmother

DATE	SOURCE	INFORMATION
/ /		Birth
/ /		Baptism
/ /		
/ /		
/ /		
/ /		
/ /		
/ /		
/ /		
/ /		
/ /		Death
/ /		Burial

Made in the USA
Monee, IL
20 February 2021

60928630R00155